EMBARRASSING

EMBARRASSING MOMENTS
IN GERMAN

and how to avoid them

**A Practical, Entertaining Guide
to Using German Correctly**

NOAH J. JACOBS

UNGAR/NEW YORK

To
WALTER AND MOLLY

1987
The Ungar Publishing Company
370 Lexington Avenue
New York, NY 10017

Fourth Printing 1987

Printed in the United States of America

Library of Congress Cataloging-in-Publication Data

Jacobs, Noah J. (Noah Jonathan), 1907–
Embarrassing moments in German, and how to avoid them.

1. German language—Errors of usage.   2. German
language—Vocabulary.   I. Title.
PF3460.J23   1987   438   87-5864
ISBN 0-8044-6309-3 (pbk.)

CONTENTS

INTRODUCTION

THE STUDENT cannot fail to notice a striking resemblance between German and English. This is not strange, for both languages have descended from a common tongue. They struck root in the same soil and for a time blossomed in the same tradition. But they soon drifted apart, each summoned to diverse tasks and to different overarching ends. The English spoken in the days of King Alfred, as late as the ninth century, had all the characteristics of modern German. Words were hooked to each other, like box-cars, by means of inflectional endings which determined their position and function in the sentence structure. The adjectives were declined, the verbs subjected to an elaborate conjugation, and every noun furnished with number, case and gender.

Then, within the space of a few centuries, a remarkable change took place in the English language. It discarded many of its grammatical forms. It dropped its subjunctive and diminutives, unsexed its nouns, and reduced its verbs to their fighting weight. At the same time the English vowels began to curdle and the words shrink, as if an astringent acid had been dropped into the language. To make matters worse, the Norman Conquest in the eleventh century imposed an alien vocabulary on the unsullied speech which had haunted the ancient English gloam. As a result of these momentous changes, the English language lost its bloated look and took on a flat, bony appearance. For example, the phrase *the noble prince who lived in the castle* can be put into the plural with surprising mobility and economy by simply adding an *s* to both nouns. In German, on the other hand, this slight change sets in motion a ponderous linguistic machinery which makes havoc of every word in the sentence: *der edle Fürst, der im Schloß wohnte* and *die edlen Fürsten, die in den Schlössern wohnten*—a dexterous piece of verbal carpentry that requires a keen eye and a steady hand. Still, despite its elaborate and noisy grammar, the German language flourished. What it lost in conciseness and flexibility it gained in architectonic beauty and formal elegance. It has even achieved some distinction in the world for its cultivated philosophical vocabulary, for the precision and resourcefulness of its technical terminology, as well as for the charm of its lowly speech and the romantic associations of its common words.

This small book is designed to give the English student an insight into the peculiar genius of the German language. It is, therefore, not primarily concerned with its morphology, its phonetic system, or the joyless details of its complicated grammar. It stresses rather those points wherein the German differs from our language and illustrates these divergencies with sentences taken from the familiar speech of the people.

I. FALSE FRIENDS

Conspicuous traces of original kinship between English and German are evident in many words which are common to both languages: arm, bitter, finger, gold, sprang, etc. The identity of the two cognates, however, is often not easily detected because of their altered forms and divergent meanings; as, *Knabe* knave, *Feind* fiend, *Tier* deer, *Zaun* town. These deviations are due to the circumstance that the original sense of the word was retained in one language and a derived or secondary meaning developed in the other. Thus, English kept the original meaning of "clean" and "foul," which was diverted in German to "small" (*klein*) and "idle" (*faul*). Conversely, in Old English "sad" had the same meaning as the corresponding modern German cognate *satt*, satiated. As early as Shakespeare's time, however, it began to be used in the present sense of mournful, for it is a common observation that one who is well-fed often tends to become calm, doleful and then sad. Similarly, the German word *glatt*, smooth, became *glad* in English, for rubbing makes things bright as well as smooth. Sometimes a foreign word entered one language in a more restricted sense than in the other, e.g. *Keks* (cookies, not cakes), *Patience* (refers in German only to the solitaire card game and not to the quality of forbearance), *prägnant* (used only in the sense of *significant import*). When the outward form as well as the inner meaning of the related words have undergone considerable change, there is no confusion since the resemblance is not readily detected; as, *Esel* easel, *Draht* thread, *Schmerz* smart, *Vieh* fee. When, however, there has been a change of meaning without a marked corresponding alteration in the outward appearance of the word, it is difficult to peer through the disguise. Such cognates are known as *False Friends:*

absolvieren. Is not "to absolve" (*von Schuld entbinden, einer Verpflichtung entheben*) but "to complete by passing an examination, to graduate from." *Er hat die Universität absolviert:* he graduated from the university.

After. Not the broad concept of "after" (*hinter*), but the very restricted meaning of "anus," the aftermost part of the body. Also: *Aftermieter:* subtenant; *Afterphilosophie:* pseudo philosophy; *Afterweisheit:* sham knowledge.

Agonie. Has not the general meaning, as in English, of intense bodily and mental pain (*Schmerz, Seelenangst*) but is restricted to the suffering before death.

Akkord. Is not "accord" (*Übereinstimmung*) but the musical "chord" (*Mehrklang*); also "piecework" (*Akkordarbeit*); *den Akkord zustande bringen, akkordieren:* to come to terms with one's creditor.

Aktion. Covers more ground than "action" (*Handlung*); *Sammelaktion:* a drive for collecting (old clothes, etc.); *Säuberungsaktion:* military mopping-up operation; political purge; a weeding out of undesirable elements; *Wohltätigkeitsaktion:* charity drive.

aktuell. Not "actual" (*wirklich*) but "timely." *Eine aktuelle Frage:* a timely subject; *der Rundfunk bringt aktuelle Nachrichten:* the radio brings up-to-date news; *das ist noch nicht aktuell:* the time is not ripe for it.

Allee. Is an "avenue lined with trees," not an "alley" (*Gäßchen*).

also. Means "so; then; therefore." *Also sei es:* so be it; *also, gut:* very well, then; *es ist also wieder so weit:* so it's come to this again; *also hat er doch recht:* he's right, after all; *es ist also doch möglich:* it is possible, say what you will.

Annonce. Is an "ad" in the papers, not an "announcement" (*Bekanntmachung, Verkündigung*).

apart. Is "distinguished, out of the ordinary." *Sie hat etwas Apartes an sich:* there is something unusual about her. On the other hand: jesting apart: *Scherz beiseite;* apart from the fact . . . : *abgesehen davon . . . ;* to take things apart: *Dinge auseinandernehmen;* I've set this day apart: *ich habe diesen Tag reserviert.*

Appell. Not "appeal" but "roll-call".

Argument. Means "proof, reason advanced," but "argument" is *Wortstreit. Die angeführten Argumente sind nicht stichhaltig:* the reasons given do not hold water.

Art. Is "manner, way" not "art" (*Kunst*). *Auf welche Art?:* How?; *Art zu verfahren:* method of procedure; *eine Art Gelehrter:* a scholar of sorts; *es liegt nicht in meiner Art:* that is not in my nature; *er ist von anderer Art:* he is of a different cast; *ein Mann seiner Art:* a man of his stamp; *er schlägt aus der Art:* he has degenerated; he's the black sheep; *Art läßt nicht von Art:* blood is thicker than water.

Artist. Means in German a "circus- or nightclub performer." "Artist" is *Künstler*, one skilled in arts in general or, in a narrower sense, *Zeichner:* draftsman.

ausgesprochen. Does not mean "outspoken" (*offenherzig*) but "pronounced, decidedly marked." *Seine ausgesprochene Absicht:* his avowed intention; *ein ausgesprochener Pessimist:* a dyed-in-the-wool pessimist; *ein ausgesprochener Bösewicht:* an out-and-out rascal; *er benahm sich ausgesprochen unverschämt:* his behavior was simply impudent; *er ist ausgesprochen einfältig:* he's as simple as they come.

bald. Means "soon," whereas "bald" is *kahl* and "a baldhead" *eine Glatze, ein Glatzkopf.*

bang. Is "afraid; worried; longing." *Es ist mir bang um ihn:* I fear for him; *es ist mir bang vor ihm:* I'm afraid of him (uneasy in his presence); *uns war angst und bang:* we were scared stiff; *mir ist bang nach ihm:* I'm longing for him. A "bang" is *ein Schlag, ein Knall;* to bang the door: *die Tür zuschlagen;* "bang!" is *bums!* "Bangs" means *Ponyfrisur.*

bekommen. Is not "become." But: what will become of me?: *was wird aus mir werden?;* it is not becoming: *es schickt sich nicht; es steht Ihnen nicht.* And: *Durst bekommen:* to grow thirsty; *Fieber bekommen:* to contract fever; *Schnupfen bekommen:* to catch cold; *Lust bekommen:* to have half a mind to; *es ist nicht zu bekommen:* it is not to be had; *wohl bekomm's!:* I hope you'll like it!; *ist es Ihnen gut bekommen?:* did it agree with you?; *die Reise ist mir gut bekommen:* I'm all the better for the trip; *es ist ihm schlecht bekommen:* it didn't do him any good; *ich kann ihn nicht zu sprechen bekommen:* I can't get to see him.

Billett. Is a ticket (for the train, theater, etc.); also a short letter, note. "Billet" is *Quartierzettel;* to billet: *ein-quartieren.*

Biskuit. Is a fine zwieback; *Biskuittorte* is a pound cake made of eggs, flour, butter and sugar. *Br.* "biscuits" (*Am.* cookies) are *Keks* (from Eng. "cakes"); "cake" is *Kuchen,* in form of a circular pie: *Torte.*

blamieren. Means "to embarrass, to make one feel foolish," not "to blame" (*beschuldigen*). *Er hat mich tüchtig blamiert:* he made me look like a fool; *du blamierst ja die Innung:* you put us to shame; *du hast dich wieder schön blamiert:* you put your foot into it again; *Mensch, blamiere dich doch nicht!:* don't act (speak) like a fool.

blank means "bright, shining, glaring." *Blank machen:* polish; *blank scheuern:* scour; *blank sein:* shine (*glänzen*), be broke (*pleite sein*); *blanker Betrug:* glaring deception; *blanke Lüge:* barefaced lie. "Blank" is *leer, unausgefüllt;* blank page: *unbeschriebenes Blatt* (also figuratively); his mind went blank: *seine Gedanken setzten plötzlich aus;* a blank shot: *ein blinder Schuß;* a blank face: *ein ausdrucksloses Gesicht;* an order blank: *ein Bestellformular.*

Born: "spring, well." "Born" is *geboren.*

Bowle. Refers to the drink which is prepared in a bowl and not to the bowl itself (*Trinkschale*). *Erdbeerbowle:* strawberry drink; *Punchbowle:* punch.

brav. Means "good, well-behaved; decent," not "brave" (*tapfer*). *Brave Kinder:* well-behaved children; *er hat brav gehandelt:* he did the right thing; *er ist ein braver Kerl:* he's a fine chap; *der brave Mann denkt an sich selbst zuletzt:* a good man thinks of himself last.

13

Brief. Is not "brief" (*kurz*) but a "letter." *Brieftasche:* wallet; *Brieffach:* pigeonhole; *Bureau für unbestellbare Briefe:* dead-letter office; *Briefkasten:* letterbox; *Briefträger:* letter carrier; *Briefmarke:* postage stamp. But, briefcase: *Aktentasche;* be brief!: *fassen Sie sich kurz!;* he was briefed: *er hat seine Instruktionen erhalten;* I hold no brief for him: *ich will ihn nicht in Schutz nehmen.*

Chef. Is the head of a firm, department, etc., somewhat like "chief." In English, however, the meaning of the word is restricted to that of the chief cook. *Bürochef:* office manager; *Abteilungschef:* head of a department; *Generalstabschef:* Chief of Staff.

Dame. Has neither the derogatory sense it has acquired in American English, nor is it used as a title for a knight's or baronet's wife as in England, but is equivalent to "lady." It is also the name of the queen in cards, chess and checkers (*Damespiel*).

denunzieren: "to inform, to squeal." *Denunziant:* informer. "To denounce" is *öffentlich anklagen*, to accuse publicly; *denunzieren* is to inform secretly.

Direktion. Besides meaning "direction," it also refers to the management of a bank, plant, etc.

Dose. Is a box, but "dose" is *Dosis*.

engagieren. Is used in the sense of "hire" (especially performing entertainers); also "to ask for a dance." *Darf ich Sie zum Tanz engagieren?:* may I have the next dance? But: I'm engaged at the moment: *ich bin momentan beschäftigt;* they were just engaged: *sie haben sich soeben verlobt.*

eventuell. Should be rendered "possibly, if need be, perhaps," but not "eventually" (*letzten Endes*). The English word refers to things which are *certain* to occur, the German to things which *may* occur. *Ich komme eventuell morgen:* chances are I'll drop in tomorrow; *Sie können mir ja eventuell Bescheid sagen:* you can let me know when you get a chance.

exerzieren. Is a military term. *Er ließ die Rekruten exerzieren:* he drilled the recruits; *Exerzierplatz:* parade grounds. "Exercise" means *Leibesübungen machen; üben.*

Existenz. Besides "existence" this word has the additional meaning of "livelihood, income." *Er hat keine sichere Existenz:* he has no steady source of income; *es war bei mir eine Existenzfrage:* my livelihood was at stake; it was a matter of life or death; *verkrachte Existenzen:* failures in life, washouts.

Fabrik. Is a "factory." "Fabric" is *Gewebe; Gefüge.*

fade. Is either "boring" (*langweilig*), or "tasteless, insipid" (*geschmacklos*). "To fade" means *verblassen.*

Fall. Has the same meaning as the English cognate, e.g., *Hochmut kommt vor dem Fall:* pride goeth before a fall. But also: *auf jeden Fall:* at all events; *auf keinen Fall:* on no account; *gesetzt den Fall:* supposing that; *schlimmsten Falles:* if worse comes to worse; *er wurde Knall und Fall entlassen:* he was fired on the spot; *das ist bei mir nicht der Fall:* that doesn't apply to me; *der erste Fall, der zweite Fall,* etc.: the nominative case, the genitive, etc.; *Fallbrücke:* drawbridge; *Fallschirm:* parachute; *Fallsucht:* epilepsy. However, *die Falle:* the trap.

famos. Both English and German borrowed this word from

the Latin *fama* in the favorable sense of "fame, renown." This meaning, however, disappeared from the German at the end of the seventeenth century and is now used in the sense of "fine, first-rate," as *ein famoser Kerl:* a fine chap, a regular fellow.

fast: "almost, nearly." *Fast nie:* hardly ever. But "fast" is *schnell;* fast sleep: *tiefer Schlaf;* fast color: *waschechte Farbe;* fast friends: *dicke Freunde;* fast women: *leichtfertige Frauen.*

fatal. Is used in German in the trivial sense of "disagreeable, annoying," unknown to English. *Eine fatale Geschichte:* an awkward affair; *ein fataler Irrtum:* an embarrassing error; *das ist fatal:* that's awfully embarrassing! that's very unfortunate. But: a fatal accident: *ein tödlicher Unglücksfall.*

fix: "quick, smart." *Ich bin fix und fertig:* I'm all set; *ich bin fix angestellt:* I've got a steady job; *außen fix, innen nix!:* all shadow and no substance. But: fixed prices: *feste Preise;* I'm in a fix: *ich bin in einer Klemme;* it's got to be fixed: *man muß es richten.*

Fleisch. English makes a distinction between the flesh of animals used for food (meat) and the soft substance between the skin and the bones of human beings (flesh). Formerly, "flesh" was used for both, as *Fleisch* is now in German, e.g. the fleshpots of Egypt: *die Fleischtöpfe Aegyptens; der Geist ist willig, aber das Fleisch ist schwach:* the spirit is willing but the flesh is weak; *sein eigenes Fleisch und Blut:* his own flesh and blood; *der Weg alles Fleisches:* the way of all flesh; *er hat sich ins eigene Fleisch* *geschnitten:* he cut off his nose to spite his face; *die Fleischwerdung Gottes:* the reincarnation of God. But: *Fleisch in Büchsen:* canned meat; *Rindfleisch:* beef; *Kalbfleisch:* veal; *Schweinefleisch:* pork.

Fonds. Is "fund, stock-in-trade, foundation"; but "be fond of" is *gern haben.* He is fond of jesting: *er macht gern Späße.*

fort. "Away, off" (*weg*); "continuously" (*weiter*). *Er ist fort:* he's away; *ich muß fort:* I must be off; *das geht so fort:* that goes on continuously this way. But "fort" is *das Fort, Festungswerk.*

Fraktion: "parliamentary faction," but "fraction" is *Bruchstück; Brocken; Bruch.*

Frauenzimmer. Is a "female" and has nothing to do with "room."

Gage. Refers to the salary of actors, officers, etc. "Gage" is *Maß; Schienenweite* and "to gage" *abschätzen.*

genial. Is "endowed with genius," not "genial" (*freundlich*) *Eine geniale Idee:* a brilliant idea; *geniale Anlagen zeigen* show marks of genius.

Gymnasium. Is a "classical high school and junior college," not a "gymnasium" (*Turnhalle*).

Hall: "sound" (*Schall*); or "resonance" (*Resonanz, Mittönen*). "Hall" is *Halle, Saal* (big room); or *Hausflur* (vestibule). "Town-hall" is *Rathaus.*

Hallo. Is not used as a greeting (except on the telephone) but rather as an exclamation to attract the attention of inattentive waiters, friends lost in a crowd, etc. It is akin to our older "halloo," formerly used to incite dogs to chase.

17

hold. Means "graceful, charming, lovely"; "hold" is *halten.*

Hose. Usually in the plural, *die Hosen:* a pair of trousers; *das Herz fiel ihm in die Hosen:* he lost his nerve. "Hose" is *Strümpfe* (stockings) or *Schlauch* (flexible pipe).

human. Is "humane." "Human" is *menschlich. Humanität* is "humaneness." "Humanity" is *das Menschengeschlecht; Humanität.* "Humanities" is *humanistische Wissenschaften;* "humanitarian" *Menschenfreund.*

Ignorant. Is "ignoramus"; *ignorieren* is "ignore." "Ignorant" is *unwissend* (unschooled) or *uninformiert* (uninformed). "Ignorance" is *Ignoranz, Unwissenheit* (lack of schooling) or *Unkenntnis* (lack of information).

Jalousie. Is not "jealousy" (*Neid*) but "Venetian blinds." *Rolljalousieschreibtisch* is "roll-top desk."

Justiz. Not "justice" (*Gerechtigkeit, Billigkeit*) but the "administration of justice."

Kadaver. Refers only to the carcass of animals, whereas "cadaver" is also used of corpses (*Leichnam*). *Kadavergehorsam:* blind obedience.

Kapazität. Besides meaning "capacity; cubic volume" this word is also used for "an eminent or highly capable personality; a scholar, a scientist."

Karton. Is "cardboard box" and not "cartoon" (*Karikatur*).

Kaution. Has retained the older meaning of "pledge, guarantee, bail" which it also had in English until the seventeenth century. *Gegen Kaution:* under bond; *Kaution stellen:* to put up bail. But: Caution! vicious dog!: *Vorsicht! Bissiger Hund.*

Klosett. Is "toilet" and not "closet" (*Schrank*).

Kolleg. Is not "college" but *Universitätsvorlesung, Universitätskurs*. *Kollege* is "colleague;" *kollegial* is "in the manner of a colleague"; *er ist im Kolleg:* he is at the lecture; *ein Kolleg belegen:* to attend a course at the university; *ein Kolleg über etwas halten:* to give a course at the university.

kompetent. Does not mean "competent" (*fähig, tüchtig*), but either *zuständig:* qualified to judge (both legally and figuratively); or *maßgebend:* authoritative, qualified to guide. *Ich bin nicht kompetent in dieser Angelegenheit:* I am not qualified to judge in this matter; *er ist mir nicht kompetent:* he is not a criterion for me (in this matter).

Konfektionär. Is a "dealer in ready-made clothes." "Confectionary" is *Konfitürengeschäft*.

Konfession. Is "faith, denomination," as *die evangelische Konfession:* the evangelical faith. "Confession" is *Geständnis; Beichte*.

Konjunktur. Is the economic situation (*die Marktlage*). *Eine günstige* (*eine schlechte*) *Konjunktur:* a favorable (an adverse) economic situation. Also: a boom (*eine Hausse*). *Eine aufgeblähte Konjunktur:* an artificial boom. But "conjuncture" is *Wendepunkt, Zusammentreffen von Umständen*.

Konkurrenz. Is "competition, rivalry"; which is the opposite of "concurrence" (*Übereinstimmung*). *Unlautere Konkurrenz:* unfair competition; *Schmutzkonkurrenz:* undercutting.

konsequent. Is "(logically) consistent." "Consequent" stresses the causal succession, ultimate results, that which follows in time. *Konsistent,* however, means "firm, compact" in a technical sense.

Konsequenz. Is "consistency," but may also mean "consequence." People of consequence: *angesehene Leute, Leute von Bedeutung. Die Konsequenzen ziehen* means "to draw one's conclusions (and act accordingly)"; *die Konsequenzen tragen* means "to take the consequences."

Konzept: "draft, sketch, rough copy." But: "concept" is *Begriff. Jemanden aus dem Konzept bringen:* confuse one; *einem das Konzept umstoßen (oder verderben):* thwart a person's schemes.

Konzern: "business combine, trust." It is a growing concern: *die Firma floriert;* it is no concern of yours: *das geht dich nichts an.*

Korn. Is 1) "grain" (*Getreide*); "rye" (*Roggen*); 2) gunsight (*Visier*): *jemanden auf dem Korn haben:* to keep an eye on someone; *aufs Korn nehmen:* to take aim at. "Corn" is *Hühnerauge* (callus on the toe); or *Br. Korn* (grain); or *Am. Mais* (maize).

Kost. "Cost" is *Kosten, Preis, Aufwand;* "to cost" *kosten. Kosten* also means "to taste, to try." *Kost* is "food" (*Nahrung*); "board" (*Verköstigung*); "diet" (*Diät*). *Feine Kost:* dainty food; *freie Kost:* free board; *Kost und Wohnung:* room and board; *leichte Kost:* light diet.

kurios. Means "odd, queer" and not "curious" (*neugierig*). *Kurioser Kauz:* queer chap. *Kuriosität* is "a curiosity" (*merkwürdiges Ding*), not "curiosity" (*Neugier*).

Kurs. Has the same meaning as "course" in: *das Schiff bleibt im Kurse:* the ship's holding her own; *der neue*

Kurs: the new trend (in politics). But: *die heutigen Kurse:* today's quotations (on the market); *wie ist der Dollarkurs?:* what's the rate of exchange for the dollar?; *außer Kurs setzen:* literally, to withdraw from circulation *(aus dem Umlauf ziehen);* figuratively, bring into disuse *(außer Gebrauch setzen).*

Last. Is a "load, burden"; *zur Last fallen:* to be a burden. But: "last": *letzte(r);* last judgment: *das jüngste Gericht;* the last meal: *Henkersmahl;* to last: *dauern, währen.*

Lektüre: "a reading," not "lecture" *(Vorlesung).* Also "reading matter" *(Lesestoff).*

List. Is "cunning"; "list" is *die Liste, das Verzeichnis.*

Lokal: "restaurant, pub; locality," not "local" *(örtlich),* as "local time": *Ortszeit. Geschäftslokal:* place of business; *Tanzlokal:* dance hall; *Lokalpatriotismus:* civic pride; also derogatorily: parochial patriotism.

Lug. Is "lookout" *(Ausguck);* or a "lie" *(Lüge)* in the phrase *Lug und Trug.* "To lug" is *schleppen.*

Luke. Is a "loophole" *(Guckloch);* "trap door" *(Falltür);* "hatch" *(Decköffnung).* "Luke" is *Lukas.*

Lump. Is "rascal" *(Gauner);* "hobo" *(Landstreicher). Lumpengesindel:* riffraff. *Er läßt sich nicht lumpen:* he's not a niggard; *nur die Lumpe sind bescheiden (Goethe):* only nobodies are modest. "Lump" is *Klumpen;* "lump sum" is *runde (auf einmal gezahlte) Summe.*

Lust. Is "lust" only in the meaning of "sensual appetite" *(Sinnenlust); seinen Lüsten frönen:* gratify one's lust. Otherwise, it means "pleasure, delight." *Ich habe Lust . . . :* I have a mind to . . . ; *ich hätte fast Lust zu . . . . :* I have

21

half a mind to . . . ; *lustlos:* listless; *Lustreise:* pleasure trip; *Lustspiel:* comedy.

Marine. Is the "German navy." But a "marine" is a *Seesoldat.* Tell that to the marines: *erzähl das deiner Großmutter.*

meinen. Is used as the equivalent of "to mean"; as, *meinen Sie das ernst?:* do you really mean it?; *er meint es gut:* he means well; *er hat es nicht böse gemeint:* he meant no harm. But also: *viele meinen, sie sei . . . :* many fancy her to be . . . ; *das will ich wohl meinen:* I quite believe; I dare say; *ich meine nur so:* I only think so; *ja, meinte er . . . :* yes, he ventured . . . ; *was meinen Sie dazu?:* what is your opinion?

Menu. Is pronounced as in French and refers generally to the actual substance of the courses more than to the bill of fare itself. Germans consume the *Menu;* we look at the "menu" (*Speisekarte*).

Minister. A member of the Cabinet; Eng. "minister" may also mean *Pfarrer* (priest).

Mist. Is not "mist" (*Nebel*) but "manure, dung" (*Dünger*), or "garbage, refuse" (*Müll*). *Der Hahn kräht auf dem Mist:* the cock crows on the dungheap; *der reine Mist:* tommyrot, pure trash; *er hat Geld wie Mist:* he's rolling in money.

Moment. There are two forms: *der Moment:* moment, instant (*Augenblick*); and *das Moment* either "import, factor, momentum" (*wichtiger Faktor*) or in physics "moment, momentum" (*Kraftwirkung*). (*Wart*) *einen Moment!:* wait a moment; *ein wichtiges Moment:* an important factor; *Moment der Trägheit:* moment of inertia.

Novelle. Is a short novel; "novel" is *Roman*. *Novelle* is also an amendment of a law. *Das Parlament nahm zu der vorgelegten Novelle Stellung:* the parliament took a stand on the proposed amendment.

ordinär. Is "low, vulgar"; not "ordinary" (*gewöhnlich, alltäglich, mittelmäßig*). *Ein ordinärer Mensch:* a cad, a vulgar fellow; *ordinärer Wein:* wine of an inferior quality.

Original. Means either "the original copy" (*Vorlage*) or a "queer chap" (*ein origineller Kauz*); or "creative personality" (*schöpferischer Mensch*). Adj. *originell* is "queer," but "original" is *schöpferisch, urwüchsig.*

Pamphlet. Is a "lampoon" or "skit" and has not the neutral meaning of "pamphlet" (*Flugschrift, Broschüre*).

Paragraph. Generally refers to a section of the legal code or document. "Paragraph" is *Absatz. Paragraphenreiter* is "stickler."

Parole. Is "watchword." *Die Parole ausgeben:* to give the password. "Parole": *Bewährungsfrist;* put on parole: *auf Ehrenwort entlassen.*

Partie. Is a "game of checkers or chess"; a "marriage match," not "party" (*Gesellschaftsabend; Partei*). *Ich bin mit von der Partie:* I'm in on it; *eine Partie ausschlagen:* to refuse a marriage offer; *Partiewaren:* seconds, slightly defective goods.

Patent. Has the same meaning as Eng. "patent," e.g., *das Patent ist abgelaufen:* the patent has expired. But: *du siehst ganz patent aus:* you look quite smart, all spruced up. "Patent" is *offen, allgemein bekannt;* patent leather: *Lackleder;* patent medicine: *Universalmedizin.*

pathetisch. In English "pathetic" is that which arouses emotions of pity or sorrow; as, a pathetic figure: *ein bemitleidenswerter Mensch*. The German *pathetisch*, however, means "solemn, pompous, with pathos." *Er trägt pathetisch vor:* he declaims with pathos.

Patron. Besides "patron" (*Beschützer, Gönner*) the German *Patron*, in Switzerland, also means "employer, boss; also, *lustiger Patron:* jolly fellow; *schlauer Patron:* shrewd customer; *windiger Patron:* windbag. But: *Patrone* is a "cartridge"; *blinde Patrone:* blank cartridge.

Pension. *Pensionieren:* to retire one on pension. *In einer Pension wohnen:* to live in a boarding house; *Pensionat:* a boarding school, generally for young ladies; *Zimmer mit Pension:* room and board.

Pest. Is "pestilence, plague." *Jemanden meiden wie die Pest:* to avoid one like a plague; *es stinkt wie die Pest:* it smells to high heaven. But: don't be a pest: *sei nicht lästig:* he is a real pest: *er ist eine wahre Landplage*.

plump. Is "awkward, clumsy," not "plump" (*mollig*). *Plump heraussagen:* to blurt out; *plumpe Schmeichelei:* gross flattery; *plumpe Lüge:* brazen lie.

positiv. Like English "positive" it may mean "affirmative" (*bejahend*): *eine positive Antwort* a positive answer. Also, *eine positive Zahl* a positive number. Otherwise, the meanings are different: *positives Wissen:* solid knowledge; *man soll nur Positives von Menschen sagen:* one should look only at the good side of people; *er nahm eine positive Haltung zu meinem Vorschlag ein:* he took a constructive attitude to my proposal. But: "positive" means *sicher,* *überzeugt.* Are you positive?: *sind Sie sicher?, wissen Sie es bestimmt?;* she is always so positive: *sie ist immer so rechthaberisch.*

pressieren. Is not "press" [*drücken* (squeeze); *bügeln* (iron)], but: *ich bin pressiert:* I'm pressed for time; *das pressiert nicht:* there's no hurry about that.

prinzipiell. "Principle" is *Prinzip,* and "principally" *hauptsächlich. Prinzipienreiter:* a stickler for principles. *Prinzipiell* may mean "in principle" (*logisch grundsätzlich*) or "on principle" (*moralisch grundsätzlich*). *Ich bin prinzipiell einverstanden:* I agree in principle; *ich tue so etwas prinzipiell nicht:* I wouldn't do such a thing on principle.

Probe. Is neither of the two English cognates: "probe" (*Prüfung,* "examination," or *Sonde,* a surgical instrument for examination) and "proof" (*Beweis*), except in the older sense; as in, *Probieren geht über Studieren:* the proof of the pudding is in the eating. *Probe* is "trial; experiment; sample; rehearsal." *Auf Probe:* on trial; *jemanden auf die Probe stellen:* to put one to the test; *Generalprobe:* dress rehearsal; *laut Probe:* as per sample; *Probearbeit:* sample of one's work.

produzieren. Besides the meaning "to produce," this word is used reflexively, e.g., *sich produzieren:* perform, (derog.) show off; *sich als Artist produzieren:* perform as a circus entertainer.

Promotion. Is "university graduation"; *promovieren:* "to take a doctor's degree." But "promotion" is *Förderung* (furtherance); *Beförderung; Werbung* (advertising and

25

publicity). The pupil was promoted: *der Schüler ist in eine höhere Klasse versetzt worden;* to promote the welfare: *die Wohlfahrt fördern.*

prompt. Is used as in English in the sense of "punctual, on time"; as *prompte Bedienung:* prompt service. But: Don't prompt!: *nicht vorsagen!;* be prompt!: *sei pünktlich!;* he answered promptly: *er hat sofort geantwortet;* prompter (in the theater): *Souffleur;* the motives which prompt me: *die Beweggründe, die mich veranlassen.*

Protektion. Is not "protection" (*Schutz*) but "patronage, pull." *Nichts geht ohne Protektion:* you can't do a thing without pull.

Provision: "commission, brokerage"; not "provision" (*Fürsorge; Vorrat; Lebensmittel*). To make provision for: *Anstalten treffen für.*

Prozeß. Is not only "process" (*das Verfahren, die Methode*) but also "trial, lawsuit." *Einem einen Prozeß anhängen:* to foist a lawsuit on a person; *der Prozeß schwebt noch:* the trial is still pending; *mit jemandem kurzen Prozeß machen:* to make short shrift of one.

Publikum. Is used in German in a more restricted sense than "public," referring to theater audiences or to the frequenters of a café. The public good: *das Gemeinwohl;* public opinion: *die öffentliche Meinung.*

Puff. Is not "puff" (*pusten, blasen, Hauch*) but "crash, thud, bang." *Er kann einen derben Puff vertragen:* he can take a beating; *es kann einen derben Puff vertragen:* it can stand rough handling. In vulgar speech *Puff* also means "brothel."

Rat. Is not "rat" (*die Ratte*) but "advice." *Rat geben:* to give advice; *zu Rate ziehen:* to consult; *jemandem mit Rat und Tat helfen:* to help one with word and deed; *keinen Rat wissen:* to be at one's wit's end; *kommt Zeit, kommt Rat:* time will find a way; we will cross that bridge when we come to it; *er weiß immer Rat:* he's never at a loss; *Frau Rat:* councillor's wife.

reell. Means not only "real" but also "solid, respectable, fair, genuine." *Ein reeller Mann:* an honest man; *reelle Ware:* a genuine article; *reelles Haus:* a sound firm; *reell bedienen:* to give good value for the money. Real money: *klingende Münze.*

Rekord. Has only the sense of "maximal achievement." *Den Rekord schlagen:* to make or break a record (*alle bisherigen Leistungen übertreffen*). Phonograph records: *Schallplatten;* we have no record of it: *wir haben keine Aufzeichnungen darüber.*

Relief. Is used only with reference to sculpture and painting in the sense of a figure projecting from the background from which it is formed. To bring into relief: *hervortreten lassen;* unemployment relief: *Unterstützung für Arbeitslose.*

Rente. Is not "rent" (*Mietgeld*), but "annuity"; *rentabel:* profitable; *rentables Geschäft:* a going concern; *er lebt von seiner Rente:* he lives on his annuity; he doesn't have to earn a living.

Residenz. Is the seat of a prince or of a court; a castle serving as a royal or princely residence. *Residenzstadt:* a town containing such a residence; *Residenztheater:* a theater attached to such a residence; the chief theater of the capital.

Ressort. (The final *t* is not pronounced, as in the French.) May be either "an administrative department of the government" or "an elastic spring." *Das gehört nicht zu meinem Ressort:* that's not in my line. A resort: *ein Kurort;* the last resort: *letzte Zuflucht;* to resort to: *seine Zuflucht nehmen zu.*

revanchieren. *Sich revanchieren* has lost the bad sense of "to retaliate, to take revenge." *Er hat keine Möglichkeit, sich zu revanchieren:* he is not in a position to reciprocate.

Rock. Is not "rock" (*Fels*) but "skirt"; "jacket." To rock: *wiegen, schaukeln.*

Routine, Rutine. Refers to "skill, dexterity," which is the result of routine practice (*gewohnheitsmäßiger Gang, Schlendrian*).

Schema. Not "scheme" (*Ränkespiel, Intrige*) but "pattern, order." *Es ging nach dem Schema F zu:* it went according to Hoyle.

selbstbewußt: Is not "self-conscious" (*verlegen, befangen*) but the opposite, i.e., "self-assured, confident."

sensibel. Means "sensitive, having tender feelings," not "sensible" (*vernünftig*).

Sentenz. Is "aphorism, maxim," more in the sense of "sententious." *In Sentenzen sprechen:* to deal in maxims or aphorisms. A "sentence" is either *Satz* (complete grammatical unit), or *Ausspruch, Urteil, Entscheidung* (judgment, decision). To sentence: *verurteilen.*

seriös: "reliable, trustworthy, honest." Seriously speaking:

im Ernst, ernstlich; serious accident: *ernster Unfall;* seriously wounded: *schwer verwundet.*

skurril. Has the original mild sense of "ludicrous, comical" (from Lat. *scurra,* buffoon), not "scurrilous" (*gemein, zotenhaft, grob verletzend*).

Smoking. Has nothing to do with the burning or inhaling of tobacco. The German borrowed this word from the English for "tuxedo" or "dinner-jacket."

So. The uses of this small but troublesome word may be illustrated by the following: *So!:* there you are!*; so?:* really?; *so,so:* middling, fair; *ach so!:* that's different; I see what you mean; *wieso?:* how's that?; *aber so etwas!:* did you ever!; *so ist es:* that's it!; *so wie so:* anyhow; *so oder so:* one way or another; *so und so viel:* a certain amount; *um so mehr:* all the more; *den so und so vielten:* such and such day of the month; *Sie sagen das nur so:* you don't mean it; *so wahr ich lebe:* as true as I stand here; *so mußte es kommen:* it was bound to happen; *er spricht bald so, bald so:* he says first one thing, then another; *die Sache ist so:* the thing's like this; *wenn dem so ist:* if that is so; *es ist nun einmal so:* that's the way it is; *wie du mir, so ich dir:* tit for tat; *so bin ich nun einmal:* I'm made that way, that's my nature; *so bist du nun:* that's you all over; *so ist er!:* that's him, that's the way he was born; *so behandeln Sie mich?:* is that the way you treat me?; *das kann nicht so bleiben:* things can't remain like this; *so fand ich ihn:* I found him in that condition; *so geht es nicht:* that won't do; *so habe ich es nicht gemeint:* I didn't mean it in that sense; *noch mal so viel:* twice as much;

29

so weit ist es gekommen: things have come to such a pass; *ist es so weit gekommen?:* has it come to this?; *so Gott will:* God willing; *so sehr er euch liebt:* much as he loves you; *so gut ich kann:* as best I can; *so viele ihrer auch sind:* however many there may be; *so viel es auch koste:* cost what it may. *Er kommt oft. So?:* He comes often. Does he? *So höre doch!:* do listen!: *er tut nur so:* he's just making believe.

solid. Is used in a more abstract sense than its English cognate. *Solide Preise:* moderate prices; *ein solides Haus:* a firm of good standing; *ein solides Leben führen:* to lead a clean, simple life; *ein solider Mensch:* a temperate, sober man.

Spektakel. Is not only "spectacle" (*Schauspiel*) but also "uproar, row" (*Krawall*).

Spleen. Has lost its more violent meaning still retained in the English "spleen" (*Verdruß, Zorn, üble Laune*). To vent one's spleen on somebody: *sein Mütchen an jemandem kühlen. Er hat einen Spleen:* he's got a screw loose.

Spur. Is "trace, vestige, scent." *Keine Spur von . . . :* not a trace of . . . "Spur" is *Sporn.* On the spur of the moment: *in der Eingebung des Augenblicks;* to spur on: *anspornen.*

Star: "starling; cataract." *Den Star stechen:* to operate for a cataract; *jemandem den Star stechen* (figuratively): to open up a person's eyes, to remove the scales from a person's eyes.

stark. Not only "strong" but also "stout, corpulent," etc. *Sie ist stark geworden:* she has become fat; *der Saal war stark besetzt:* the lecture was well-attended; *eine starke*

Klasse: a large class; *starkes Fieber:* high fever; *starke Kälte:* severe cold; *starker Regen:* heavy rain; *starker Wind:* high wind; *starker Spaß:* coarse joke; *das ist stark:* that's strong stuff. But: stark blind: *stockblind;* stark mad: *ganz verrückt;* stark naked: *splitternackt.*

Stipendium. Is a "scholarship," not a "stipend" (*Lohn, Gehalt*).

sympathisch. "Sympathetic" has retained the more original meaning of "having a fellow-feeling for others." He deserves sympathy: *er ist bemitleidenswert.* The German word merely means "nice, likeable." *Ein sympathischer Mensch:* a likeable fellow; *es berührt mich sympathisch:* it strikes a responsive chord in me.

Tip. "Tip" is *Trinkgeld,* but *jemandem einen Tip geben* is "to give someone advance, secret information on the races, market, etc.," which is also one of the meanings of the word in English. The German *Type* is the same as the English type (for printing). *Typ* (abbreviation of *Typus*) is "example, model, character." *Type, Typus, Typ* are all "type" in English. However, *die Type* is the type for printing, while *der Typus* or *Typ* means "kind" (*Art*). *Er ist ein ganz anderer Typ:* he is a very different kind of man.

toll. "Toll" (*Wegzoll; Glockengeläute*), but *toll* is "mad." *Es ging toll her:* it was a riot; *das Tollste dabei ist . . . :* the funniest part about it is . . . ; *das ist das Tollste, was ich je gehört habe:* that beats everything I've ever heard; *es toll treiben:* to exceed all bounds; *Tollwut:* hydrophobia, rabies; *tollkühn:* foolhardy; *Tollhaus:* insane asylum; *Tollhäusler:* lunatic, madman.

Ton. *Den Ton angeben:* to set the fashion; *ein Mann von gutem Ton:* a well-bred gentleman; *tonangebende Kreise:* fashionable circles; *das gehört zum guten Ton:* that is a mark of good breeding; *der Ton macht die Musik:* it's not what you say but how you say it; *Kasernenton:* the imperious, raucous voice of an army sergeant.

überhören. Is not "to overhear" (*zufällig mitanhören*) but "to fail to hear." *Ich habe die letzten Worte überhört:* I didn't catch your last words.

Waggon. Is stressed on the last syllable and means "a railway coach" and not a "wagon" (*Wagen*).

Wink. "To wink" (*mit den Augen blinzeln, zwinkern*); to wink at a person: *jemandem zuzwinkern;* forty winks after lunch: *Mittagsschläfchen.* But: *mit der Hand winken:* to wave; *jemandem einen Wink mit dem Zaunpfahl geben:* to give one a broad hint; *sie folgen ihm auf den Wink:* they're at his beck and call; *ein sanfter Wink:* a gentle reminder; *in einem Wink:* in a jiffy; *kein Wink von ihm:* no trace of him.

Zylinder. Besides the meaning of "cylinder" this word also means a "top hat." *Lampenzylinder:* lamp chimney.

II. THE GENIUS OF THE GERMAN LANGUAGE

The language a nation speaks is the unique reflection of its genius. This genius does not proceed from a fixed authority but is guided in its labors by a *Sprachgefühl* which adopts and rejects forms in accordance with its own subtle dictates. It is therefore difficult, if not impossible, to be bilingual or to render a word adequately from one language into another. English and German, for example, had a common source but soon parted company, each following its own bent. In the course of time the living words of the two languages became tainted with alien associations and rallied around different unifying cores.

The German language has inflexibly pursued its own course, concerned with the fulfillment of its own destiny. It is oriented towards its own beckoning goals which reflect German character and temperament. The German language occupies the fourth place among world languages, being surpassed in the number of its speakers only by Chinese, English and Russian. It is distinguished by the following characteristics:

1. THE FORMATION OF NEW WORDS:
German forms its words, as English did before the Norman Conquest, out of its own resources, by a kind of inbreeding. The two chief ways it employs to extend its vocabulary are by composition (*Zusammensetzung*) to form

compounds and by derivation (*Ableitung*) by means of prefixes and suffixes to form derivatives.

COMPOUNDS BY COMPOSITION

a. two nouns compounded: *Dollarlücke:* dollar gap; *Währungsumstellung:* currency reform; *Luftschutzkeller:* air raid shelter. *Kriegsversorgungsgesetz:* Law on Pensions to War Victims.

b. adjective plus noun: *Hochhaus:* skyscraper; *Hochmut:* arrogance; *Kleingeld:* small change; *Süßstoff:* saccharine; *Fertighaus:* pre-fab; *Kurzschluß:* short circuit.

c. verb stem plus noun: *Sitzkrieg:* phony war; *Leihhaus:* pawn shop; *Bückwaren:* under-the-counter goods.

d. noun plus adjective to form adjectives: *schalldicht:* soundproof; *kußfest:* kissproof; *wasserdicht:* waterproof; *weltfremd:* naive; *verwandlungsfähig:* chameleonlike.

e. prefixes to form compound verbs: *aufpulvern:* to pep up; *sich austoben:* to sow one's wild oats; *mitarbeiten:* to collaborate; *abwimmeln:* to get rid of.

f. noun clusters: *das Zuhörenkönnen:* the ability to listen; *das Ausderrollefallen:* acting out of character; *das sich Nichtausschlafenkönnen:* the inability to get enough sleep; *das Übersichhinauswachsenwollen:* the urge to accomplish something beyond one's capabilities.

COMPOUNDS BY DERIVATION

a. *Nouns:*

-er   *-er* may be added not only to indicate a personal agent, as; *Geldpolitiker:* one who is concerned with monetary policy, or to indicate the inhabitant of a city, as *Berliner*, *Kölner*, but also to indicate instrument or means, as *Roller:* scooter; *Stecker:* plug; *Wecker:* alarm clock.

Note that in English the suffix -er may indicate persons of both sexes; in German only male persons. In order to indicate a female person we have to add another suffix *-in.* "The dreamer" may mean *der Träumer* and *die Träumerin.* "Beautiful dreamer" suggests to the German at first invariably a dreaming young man.

-ung   *Tarnung:* camouflage; *Schiebung:* black-market and other shady transaction; *Verdeutschung:* translation into German.

-schaft *Studentenschaft:* student body; *Lehrerschaft:* teaching staff at a secondary school; *Genossenschaft:* co-operative; *Knappschaft:* miners' lodge; *Kundschaft:* clientele.

-erei   This suffix has often a derogatory meaning, indicating frequently something troublesome or unnecessarily complicated, as: *Schererei:* fuss; *Wortklauberei:* hairsplitting; *Parteigängerei:* political factionalism; *Schweinerei:* skulduggery, dirty mess; *Kurpfuscherei:* quackery. However, referring to crafts and their shops, *-erei* has a perfectly neutral implication: *Bäckerei:* bakery (shop); *Tischlerei:* carpentry (shop); *Schneiderei:* tailory.

b. adjectives:

-ig *gesprächig:* talkative; *mollig:* plump; *wendig:* manoeuvrable; *patzig:* arrogant, bossy; *schlampig:* sloppy; *schneidig:* smart, trim.

-lich *kleinlich:* petty; *tunlich:* feasible; *gründlich:* thorough; *überheblich:* arrogant.

-erisch *prahlerisch:* boastful; *geheimtuerisch:* putting on an air of secrecy; *großtuerisch:* swaggering; *halsbrecherisch:* breakneck.

-bar *unübersetzbar:* untranslatable; *befliegbar:* accessible by plane; *schiffbar:* navigable; *eßbar:* edible.

Letter words:

Schupo (*Schutzpolizei:* policeman); Sipo (*Sicherheitspolizei:* security police); Gestapo (*geheime Staatspolizei:* G-men); Flak (*Fliegerabwehrkanone:* antiaircraft gun); Pak (*Panzerabwehrkanone:* antitank gun); VGV (*Verwaltung der gesperrten Vermögen:* Blocked Properties Administration); ABP (*Arbeitsbeschaffungsprogramm:* Works Creation Program); BGH (*Bundesgerichtshof:* Federal Supreme Court); BAM (*Bundesarbeitsministerium:* Federal Ministry of Labor).

2. This tendency to form words by incest makes the German vocabulary more easily understood by both native and foreigner. Whereas English words, such as; ruminant, carburetor, oval, dactylology, hippopotamus or skunk are more or less obscure, the German equivalen s are dead giveaways: *Wiederkäuer, Vergaser, eiförmig, F ge sprache,*

36

Nilpferd and *Stinktier*. As a result of this centripetal force in the language, Germans prefer the home-made compound to the foreign import, *Fremdwörter*—a tendency fostered by language patriots banded together in powerful societies, *Sprachvereine*. For example, *Abteil* is preferable to *Coupé*, *Aufschneider* to *Renommist*, *Bahnsteig* to *Perron*, *Briefwechsel* to *Korrespondenz*, *malerisch* to *pittoresk*, *Schnellzug* to *Expreß*, *Tierarzt* to *Veterinär*, *Wortschatz* to *Vokabular*, *Zweigstelle* to *Filiale*, *Spähtrupp* to *Patrouille*.

Some of these foreign words, however, which have escaped the purists (*Sprachreiniger*), are no longer felt as aliens and have been fully assimilated into the language, e.g., *Kultur, Idee, Genie, Technik, Charakter, Industrie*.

Words that have come into the German as a result of a piece-by-piece translation from another language are known as *Lehnübersetzungen* (loan translations), e.g., *Vorurteil* (*L. praeiudicium*), *Gesichtspunkt* (*Fr. point de vue*), *Gewissen* (*L. con-scire*), *Lautsprecher* (loudspeaker), *Jungfernrede* (maiden speech), *Leitartikel* (leading article), *meine bessere Hälfte* (my better half), *der allmächtige Dollar* (the almighty dollar). When the meaning of a native word is extended under the influence of foreign usage, we have *Lehnbedeutung* (semantic loan), e.g., *einen schneiden* (to snub one), influenced by the Eng. to "cut one socially."

3. German makes a distinction between separable verbs (which stress the prefix, as *ab'fahren*) and inseparable verbs (which stress the root, as *verges'sen*). The former give us such sentences as: *Er sah ihn verblüfft an:* he looked at him

nonplussed; *er wich dem Hund aus:* he went out of the dog's way; *er brach mit schnellem Entschluß die Brücken hinter sich ab:* he quickly resolved to burn the bridges behind him.

Some verbs are both separable and inseparable, like the English "overtake" and "take over." When *übersetzen,* for example, is inseparable it is used in the sense "to translate"; when separable, it is used in the sense of "to move across (the river)." *Ich überset'ze das Buch. Das Buch ist zu überset'zen. Das Buch ist übersetzt' worden.* But: *Ich setze die Truppen ü'ber. Die Truppen sind ü'berzusetzen. Die Truppen sind ü'bergesetzt worden.*

4. German has retained its complicated grammatical machinery and highly inflected character. Its irrational, capricious gender, for example, which bears no relation to sex, seems to be but a useless burden to the memory. Sense is no guide to gender: *der Arm, die Hand, das Knie; der Löffel, die Gabel, das Messer; der Anfang, die Mitte, das Ende; der Wolf, die Katze, das Schwein.* A masculine noun may indicate both sexes (*der Sperling*), as may a feminine noun (*die Maus*), or a neuter (*das Pferd*); a feminine noun may refer to a male (*die Schildwache:* the sentry) or to a neuter (*die Frucht*), a masculine noun to a female (*der Weisel:* the queen bee), or to a neuter (*der Tisch*), and a neuter may refer to a female (*das Weib*).

Because of its highly inflected character, a German sentence may begin with any one of the four cases: *Den Faust* (accusative, masc., sing.) *hatte Goethe immer bei sich.*

Unbefugten (dative, plur.) *ist der Zutritt verboten. Der deutschen Kunst* (dative, fem., sing.) *gewidmet. Der langen Rede* (genitive, fem., sing.) *kurzer Sinn* (nominative, masc. sing.). *Der Widerspenstigen* (genitive, fem., sing.) *Zähmung. Des Knaben* (genitive, masc., sing.) *Wunderhorn* (the title of a famous anthology of *Volkslieder*, 1806). *Das Wunder ist des Glaubens liebstes Kind* (nominative, neut., sing.).

For the same reason the noun may be removed from the article: *Ein Muezzin ist einer, der von einer innerhalb der Moschee errichteten Tribüne aus fünfmal täglich die Aufforderung zum Gebet singt:* A muezzin is one who sings forth the call to prayer five times daily from an elevated platform erected inside the mosque. *Eine Mumie ist eine durch natürliche Austrocknung oder künstliche Zubereitung vor Verwesung geschützte Leiche:* A mummy is a corpse which is protected against putrefaction by natural desiccation or by artificial preparation. *Ein von einer deutschen Telegraphenanstalt nach New York auf dem Funkweg befördertes Telegramm kostet gegenwärtig 2 RM je Wort:* The present rate for telegrams sent by wireless from a German telegraph office to New York is 2 marks per word.

These structural divergencies between German and English are aggravated by differences in the history and outlook of the speakers of both languages. Thus, we have words in English not found in German, for the things they represent are unknown to the latter, as: truant officer, spelling bee, Jim Crow, hot foot, or Bronx cheer. Or, having the thing, the genius of the German language has not yet

39

devised a word for it, e.g.: blind date, Dutch treat, spring fever, sugar daddy.

Conversely, we find things in German unknown to English, as: *Duzbruder:* a friend who may be addressed by the familair form *du; Fidibus:* a long paper match used by students to light their pipes; *Föhn:* a warm, dry westwind from the Alps, which produces discomfort to man and beast, especially in South Germany; *Hitzferien:* school holidays because of unbearable heat; *Litfaßsäule:* cylindrical billboard seen in European cities (named after *Litfaß,* who introduced them in Berlin around 1860); *Studentenfutter:* a mixture of almonds, figs, nuts and raisins; *Vesper* (in Vienna *Jause;* in Switzerland *z'Vieri* or *z'Abig*): a four o'clock snack.

Or, if the English is familiar with the thing, it has yet found no apt phrase or formal expression for it. Examples of these are such typical German words, as:

Backfisch: a self-conscious adolescent girl in the awkward age. Not a flapper, which has the connotation of coquette; nor bobby-soxer, which is a spirited, "sophisticated" girl alien to German. (The name is derived from the young fish which are good for baking (*Backen*) but not for cooking).

Binsenwahrheit: truism or self-evident truth. (Perhaps because such truths are as thin and meager as *Binsen,* rushes).

Einfall: a sudden idea.

Fingerspitzengefühl: an intuitive flair; a fine, natural sense.

Galgenhumor: reckless merriment in the shadow of the gallows; humor at one's own expense.

Gardinenpredigt: a private chiding administered by a wife to her husband.

Geltungsbedürfnis: the need for prestige and self-assertion.

Gemütlichkeit: genial informality (of a person); coziness (of atmosphere).

Geschichtsklitterung: historical writing which consciously distorts facts.

Henkersmahl: the last meal given to one condemned to death.

Kannegießer: beerhouse politician; armchair politician.

Kinderstube (fig.): good breeding, savoir-vivre. *Er hat keine Kinderstube:* his manners are poor.

Kitsch (adj. *kitschig*): sentimental trash; tawdry, lowbrow art.

Landpomeranze: female country bumpkin; a female hick.

Milchmädchenrechnung: a highly speculative calculation based on deceptive assumptions.

Mumienschänder: a young man who cultivates the friendship of elderly women (the opposite of "cradle snatcher").

Potemkinsche Dörfer: a deceptive, illusory, camouflaged view (from Potemkin, who hurriedly erected seemingly populated towns to give Catherine II a false view of the country).

Radfahrertypus: a familiar type who kowtows to his superiors and at the same time browbeats those under him.

Reisefieber: the feverish anticipation before starting on a journey.

Schadenfreude: malicious joy at another's discomfort.

Stammgast: a steady customer of a restaurant or café and one who generally occupies the same table (*Stammtisch*).

sturmfreie Bude: a room with a private entrance, removed from prurient gaze, and coveted by bachelors.

Stimmvieh: a voter who is a political ignoramus.

Treppenwitz: esprit d'escalier; a telling retort too late thought of (a witty afterthought that occurs to one on the way down the stairs).

Tücke des Objekts (from Friedrich Theodor Vischer's novel *Auch Einer* 1879): the way things have of annoying us, the revenge of inanimate objects, the cussedness of things.

Zeitgeist: the collective way of thinking of a given period, the ruling ideas of an age.

Zivilcourage: moral courage as distinct from that displayed on the battlefield. (The word was coined by Bismarck as a reproach to his countrymen.)

On the whole, however, and often with surprising accuracy the expressions of one language get themselves somehow translated into the other:

Altweibersommer: Indian summer; *Amtsschimmel:* red tape; *Anstandswauwau:* chaperon; *Basiliskenblicke:* dagger looks; *Blütezeit:* golden period, heyday; *Bonze:* political or union big shot; *Bratkartoffel:* German fried; *Drückeberger:* slacker; *Engpaß:* bottleneck; *Hochstapler:* fourflusher; *Lampenfieber:* stage fright; *er hat O-Beine (X-Beine):* he is bowlegged (knock-kneed); *Nassauer:* sponger; *Nepplokal:*

gyp joint; *Pechvogel:* unlucky bird, one who has the jinx; *Scharfmacher:* get-tough advocate; *Schmerbauch:* bay window; *Schmöker: (alter Band)* old tome; *(Schundbuch)* trashy book; *schmökern:* browse about among books; *ein Schuldschein:* an IOU; *Waschzettel:* a blurb.

Battle-axe: *eine böse Sieben;* debunk: *eines falschen Nimbus entkleiden;* debunk Napoleon: *Napoleon in Unterhosen zeigen;* gold digger: *Männerausbeuterin, Mädel vom Stamme Nimm;* go-getter: *Draufgänger;* hick: *Jokel;* rabble rouser: *Hetzer;* road hog: *Landstraßenschreck;* red herring: *Ablenkungsmanöver;* rubber check: *geplatzter Scheck;* shyster: *Winkeladvokat;* stool pigeon: *Lockspitzel;* sucker: *Gimpel, Wurzen;* ticket scalper: *Agioteur, wilder Billethändler;* underdog: *der Schwächere;* showdown: *entscheidende Auseinandersetzung.*

Man traverses the whole domain of thought with the seven-league boots of his imagination, travelling farther than Columbus and discovering lordlier realms. The arbitrary associations of his fantasy are restrained only by the lexical and phonetic resources at his disposal. For example, we often detect a disconcerting similarity, real or fancied, between the beasts of the field and ourselves. In the nature of things, the same animal trait will commend itself to the imagination in all languages and be related by analogy to man's social life. Both English and German, for example, discern the same mournful revelation in our lowly origin:

Gänsehaut: goose pimples; *Hundsfott:* a cur; *Ziegenbart:*

a goatee; *Salonlöwe:* social lion; *hundemüde:* dog-tired; *vor die Hunde gehen:* go to the dogs; *aalglatt:* slippery as an eel; *nachäffen:* to ape; *wie Hund und Katze leben:* get along like cat and dog; *fromm wie ein Lamm:* meek as a lamb; *ein geiler Hund:* a lascivious dog; *arm wie eine Kirchenmaus:* poor as a churchmouse; *einen Bärenhunger haben:* be hungry as a bear.

The two languages, however, often make diverse analogies, as:

stumm wie ein Fisch: close as a clam; *gesund wie ein Fisch im Wasser:* sound as a roach, (roach: *Plötze*, a fish), fit as a fiddle; *ein netter Käfer:* a cute trick (of a girl); *Versuchskaninchen:* guinea pig; *Hasenfuß:* chicken heart; *die Katze im Sacke kaufen:* buy the pig in the poke; *eine süße Maus:* a sweetie pie; *ochsen:* bone, cram; *Blindekuh:* blindman's buff; *munter wie eine Schwalbe:* gay as a lark; *Schwein haben:* have good luck; *faule Fische:* lame excuses; *faule Fische und Schläge dazu!* that's insult added to injury.

The things of this world, however, are so myriad and the possible relations so manifold that it is not to be expected that the strange workings of the imagination should make the same distinctions or stumble upon the same combinations. Thus, the German exhibits a strange fondness for the rank-smelling goat, from which it derives: *Ziegenpeter:* the mumps; *einen Bock schießen:* pull a boner; *ins Bockshorn jagen:* browbeat. And from the parasitic louse it took: *ihm ist eine Laus über die Leber gelaufen:* he is cross, disgruntled; *er hat mir eine Laus in den Pelz gesetzt:*

he saddled me with an annoying companion. The sting has been somewhat removed from that troublesome insect in *Lausbub,* which the Germans often use as a term of endearment, like "rascal." Originally it means a (lousy) hoodlum.

Both languages derived expressions from the "horse." The English has: horseplay: *der derbe Scherz;* horse laugh: *wieherndes Gelächter;* horse-radish: *Meerrettich;* horse sense: *der gesunde Menschenverstand;* a Charley horse: *ein Muskelkater in den Schenkeln;* straight from the horse's mouth: *aus erster Quelle;* that's a horse of another color: *das ist eine ganz andere Geschichte;* put the cart before the horse: *das Pferd beim Schwanz aufzäumen.* The German has: *Pferdekur (Roßkur):* a drastic cure; *sich vergaloppieren:* let one's arguments run away with one; *über die Stränge schlagen:* kick over the traces; *wenn alle Stränge reißen:* if worse comes to worse. From "cat" the English derives "catty" (*katzengleich*), "cat's-paw" (*willenloses Werkzeug*) and "pussyfooting" (*Leisetreterei*). The Germans, however, saw much more in this soft-furred, mice-pursuing, domestic animal: *Katzengold:* false gold; *Katzenmusik:* charivari; bronx cheer; *Katzensprung:* a stone's throw; *katzenfreundlich:* hypocritically friendly; *Katzelmacher:* humorous designation for an Italian; *jemandem einen Katzenkopf geben:* to give one a box on the ear; *Geldkatze:* money pouch; *Katzenjammer:* hangover; *katzbuckeln:* to kowtow, cringe; *das ist für die Katz:* that's of no earthly use; *bei Nacht sind alle Katzen grau:* all cats are gray by night.

English has two words for the simians, monkey and ape. The German gets along with one word *Affe.* Ape:

45

nachäffen; monkey with: *herumpfuschen;* monkey around: *sich unnütz oder geschäftig machen;* monkey tricks: *Narrenspossen;* monkey business: *Dreh; Unfug;* monkey wrench: *englischer Schlüssel, Universalschraubenschlüssel; Nachäffer:* copycat; *Affenliebe:* doting, over-indulgent love; *Affenschande:* a dirty shame; *Affenschwanz:* an ass, a fool; *Affennase:* a snub nose; *Affentheater:* (monkey) circus; *er hat einen Affen:* he's drunk; *sie hat einen Affen an ihm gefressen:* she is infatuated with him.

The English has not done much with "hen": a henpecked husband: *ein Pantoffelheld;* a hen party: *ein Kaffeekränzchen;* scarce as hen's teeth: *sehr rar.* On the other hand, the German has elaborated on that ill-tempered fowl for which it has three words: *das Huhn* (diminutive *Hühnchen*), the masculine *Hahn* (rooster), and the feminine *Henne* (hen). *Ein verrücktes Huhn:* a screwball; *ein blindes Huhn findet auch mal ein Körnchen:* even the poorest shot has his lucky day; *ich habe ein Hühnchen mit Ihnen zu rupfen:* I've a bone to pick with you; *Hühnerblindheit:* night blindness; *da lachen ja die Hühner:* that gives one a horse laugh; *Hühnerstiege:* steep stairs; *mit den Hühnern zu Bett gehen:* to go to bed with the chickens; *Hühneraugen:* corns (on the toes); *er ist Hahn im Korb:* he's the cock of the walk; *jemandem den roten Hahn aufs Dach setzen:* to set someone's house on fire; *es kräht kein Hahn danach:* no one gives a hoot about it; *(Wasser)hahn:* the tap, faucet; *(Gas)hahn:* (gas) cock; *den Hahn spannen:* cock a gun; *Hahnrei:* cuckold.

Parts of the body are another favorite source of

analogies. The German has: *einem die Stirn bieten:* to stand up to one; *er hat die Stirne, mir so etwas zu sagen:* he has the nerve to tell me that; *es steht ihm an der Stirn geschrieben:* it's written all over him. Similarly, with "ear": *jemandem einen Floh ins Ohr setzen:* put a bee in one's bonnet; *ganz Ohr sein:* be all ears; *die Ohren spitzen:* prick up one's ears; *er hat es faustdick hinter den Ohren:* he's a clever rascal; *sich etwas hinter die Ohren schreiben:* take something to heart; *Ohrfeige:* box on the ear; *Ohrenbläser:* talebearer (*Zwischenträger*); mealymouth (*Schmeichler*).

Both languages have been more successful with "nose" and "foot." Nosey: *neugierig;* nose about: *herumspähen;* a nose dive: *ein Sturzflug;* count noses: *Stimmen zählen;* pay through the nose: *tüchtig blechen.* But: *näseln:* speak through the nose; *naseweis:* smart-alecky; *hochnäsig:* snooty; *er hat sich eine Nase geholt:* he was called up on the carpet; *ich sehe es dir an der Nase an:* it's written all over your face; *ich werde es dir nicht an die Nase binden:* I don't mean to tell it to you right off; *ich habe ihm die Würmer aus der Nase ziehen müssen:* I had to worm it out of him; *sie hat es ihm unter die Nase gerieben:* she cast it in his teeth, she rubbed it in; *ich habe die Nase voll:* I'm fed up; *einem auf der Nase herumtanzen:* step all over one; *mit langer Nase abziehen:* to go off peeved; *die Nase hängen lassen:* be dejected.

Similarly with "foot": put one's foot down: *energisch handeln;* put one's foot in: *sich blamieren;* foot the bill: *die Rechnung bezahlen;* before the footlights: *im Rampenlicht;* foothold: *Stützpunkt;* foothills: *Vorgebirge.* But: *Zinsfuß:* rate of interest; *Fußboden:* floor; *trockenen Fußes:* dry-shod;

47

stehenden Fußes: immediately; *auf großem Fuße leben:* to live in grand style; *auf freiem Fuße:* at liberty, at large; *auf gutem (gespanntem) Fuß mit jemandem stehen:* be on good terms (have strained relations) with someone; *auf schwachen Füßen stehen:* be shaky; *die Sache hat weder Hand noch Fuß:* there's no rhyme or reason to it; *sie wehrte sich mit Händen und Füßen:* she defended herself tooth and nail.

Each language, then, seizes upon some obvious image from the storehouse of its inner speech form, and by analogy relates it to the world without. Arbitrary combinations are made from the view of a language's private bias and the nature of its linguistic equipment. The desire for alliteration, for example, must avail itself of the phonetic peculiarities at a language's disposal:

Krethi und Plethi: every Tom, Dick and Harry; *mit allem Drum und Dran:* the whole shebang; *mag es biegen oder brechen:* by hook or crook; *mit Kind und Kegel:* with bag and baggage; *eine Zeit des Hangens und Bangens:* a harrowing time, a time that tries men's souls; *in Hülle und Fülle:* enough and to spare; *das ist erstunken und erlogen:* that's a filthy lie; *von Pontius zu Pilatus:* from pillar to post.

The two languages often adopt the same classical and Biblical reference: jovial: *jovial;* laconic: *lakonisch;* St. Vitus dance: *Veitstanz;* Achilles' heel: *Achillesferse;* Caesarian section: *Kaiserschnitt;* jeremiad: *Jeremiade.*

Sometimes the German derives words from classical

sources not found in the English, as: *katonische Strenge:* the severity of a martinet; *Tituskopf:* a head with short, frizzled hair; *Lukullusmahl:* a dinner from soup to nuts; *Eulen nach Athen tragen:* to bring coal to Newcastle; *Philistertum:* Philistinism, babbittry; *Hiobsbote:* bringer of bad news; *den alten Adam ausziehen:* to turn over a new leaf.

The two languages may also differ in the use of place names as adjectives: *Berlinerblau:* Prussian blue; *die englische Krankheit:* the rickets; *ein Engländer:* a monkey wrench; *englisches Salz:* Epsom salts; *Englischpflaster:* court plaster; *spanische Wand:* folding screen; *das kommt mir spanisch vor* (or: *das sind mir böhmische Dörfer*)*:* that's all Greek to me; *Jägerlatein:* huntsman's yarns, fish story; *hier geht mein Latein zu Ende:* I am at my wit's end.

There are also differences in proper names used in a transferred sense: *den dicken Wilhelm spielen:* to throw one's weight around; *der deutsche Michel:* Michel (night-capped symbol of the simple-minded but forthright German); *Heulsuse:* Calamity Jane; *die grüne Minna* or *der grüne Heinrich:* the black Maria (police wagon). The German has naturally seized upon the common name *Hans* to form many expressions: *Hans Dampf in allen Gassen:* a busybody, a rubberneck (after a novel by Heinrich Zschokke 1854); *Hätschelhans:* a spoiled brat; *Hans im Glück:*Hans in Luck (fairy tale of a lad who exchanges his burdensome lump of gold for increasingly worthless things); *Hansnarr:* tomfool; *Hanswurst:* merry andrew; *Prahlhans:* braggart; *dort ist Schmalhans Küchenmeister:* they live on short rations there.

Or, a language may show a preference for a certain structural peculiarity, alien to another language. For example, compound words formed in German with *Not*: *Notlage:* sorry plight, distress; *Notstandsgebiet:* distressed area; *Notverordnung:* emergency decree; *Notausgang:* emergency exit; *Notauswurf:* jetsam; *Notbau:* temporary structure; *Notgeld:* paper money in crises; *Notlüge:* white lie; *Notbedarf:* necessities; *Notpfennig:* savings put by for a rainy day; *Notverband:* temporary dressing; *Notwehr:* self-defense; *Notsitz:* rumble seat; *Notbehelf:* makeshift; *Notbremse:* emergency brake; *Nottreppe:* fire escape; *Notflagge:* flag of distress; *Notruf:* emergency call, distress signal; *Nothafen:* harbor of refuge; *Notzucht:* rape. Besides these, German is fond of the word *Not* in common expressions: *wenn Not am Mann ist:* if worse comes to worse; *in großer Not sein:* to be hard up; *mit knapper Not davonkommen:* escape by the skin of one's teeth; *mit der Not kämpfen:* keep the wolf from the door; *Not ist der Liebe Tod:* when poverty comes in at the door, love flies out at the window; *aus der Not eine Tugend machen:* to make a virtue out of necessity; *mit Mühe und Not:* just barely; *Not kennt kein Gebot:* necessity knows no law; *in der Not frißt der Teufel Fliegen:* any port is good in a storm.

III. VERBAL JACKS-OF-ALL-TRADES

In English the same word is often summoned to perform different functions in the sentence, as: *a can, to can, canned meat.* By establishing rigid traffic rules of word order English is thus able to shift its words, like mobile infantry, from one task to another with a minimum of confusion and with admirable economy. The word *round*, for example, may serve as a noun, verb, adjective, adverb and preposition; *still* as a noun, verb, adjective, adverb and conjunction. The ability of such words to play several syntactical roles in the sentence has enriched our language with a bewildering number of idiomatic expressions which are difficult to render into another language: an also-ran, outherod, isms, happy-go-lucky, etc. The chief troubleshooters are the small but strong words GET, PUT, MIND, MAKE, DO, GO, RUN, KEEP, TAKE, UP and OFF.

get:

Get + noun:

He got bad breaks: *er hat Pech gehabt;* that gets my goat: *das bringt mich in Zorn;* I can't get the hang of it: *ich kann den Kniff nicht herausbekommen;* I get a kick out of it: *das macht mir großen Spaß;* I've got his number: *ich habe ihn durchschaut;* I can't get a word in edgewise: *ich kann nicht zu Wort kommen;* you've got something there!: *was du sagst, hat manches für sich.*

Get + adverbial phrase:

He got away by the skin of his teeth: *er kam mit*

knapper Not davon; he gets away with murder: *er kann sich alles erlauben (ohne daß ihm etwas passiert);* let's get down to brass tacks: *kommen wir zur Sache!;* he got up on the wrong side: *er ist mit dem linken Fuß zuerst aufgestanden;* we're getting nowhere fast: *wir dreschen leeres Stroh;* you've got me there!: *jetzt weiß ich dir nichts zu erwidern.*

Get + it:

I've got it down pat now: *ich hab's jetzt im Griff;* he's got it in for me: *er hat es scharf auf mich;* he had to get it out of his system: *er mußte sich davon befreien;* let's get it over with!: *schauen wir, daß wir's hinter uns kriegen!;* he got it in the neck: *er hat eins aufs Dach gekriegt;* don't let it get you!: *machen Sie sich nichts daraus!, Mensch, ärgere dich nicht!*

And: she's got a funny get-up on: *sie ist komisch aufgestutzt;* he made a quick getaway: *er türmte, er nahm die Füße in die Hand;* he's a go-getter: *er ist ein Draufgänger;* you've got to hand it to him: *das muß man ihm lassen;* they've got what it takes: *sie haben das Zeug dazu.*

put:

I wouldn't put it past him: *das traue ich ihm schon zu;* put it there: *schlag ein!—abgemacht;* he's putting it on: *er produziert sich nur;* now, stay put: *jetzt mucks dich aber ja nicht!*

mind:

Mind the baby: *paß auf das Kind auf!;* never mind!: *das macht nichts!;* do you mind?: *haben Sie etwas dagegen?;* mind your p's and q's!: *passen Sie sehr gut auf; seien Sie sehr bedachtsam (in Ihrem Verhalten)!;* mind your own business!: *kümmern Sie sich um Ihre eigenen Angelegenheiten;* he's absent-minded: *er ist zerstreut;* I gave her a piece of my mind: *ich habe ihr gehörig Bescheid gesagt;* my mind's not at ease: *ich bin unruhig;* I see it in my mind's eye: *ich sehe es im Geiste;* he had presence of mind: *er besaß Geistesgegenwart;* keep me in mind: *denk an mich!;* to my mind . . . : *für mein Gefühl . . .*

make:

How did you make out?: *wie hast du abgeschnitten?;* he couldn't make her: *er hat keine Chancen bei ihr;* she's on the make: *sie sucht Anschluß; sie ist auf Männerfang aus;* she forgot to put her make-up on: *sie hat vergessen, sich zurechtzumachen;* he made his pile: *er hat sein Schäfchen im Trockenen;* it made me cry: *ich mußte weinen;* make-believe: *Vortäuschung;* makeshift: *Notbehelf.*

come:

She just came to: *sie kam eben wieder zu sich;* when it comes to looks, . . . : *was sein Aussehen anlangt, . . . ;* he has it coming to him: *er verdient es nicht anders;* come to think of it . . . : *was ich noch sagen wollte . . . ;* it doesn't come up to scratch: *das entspricht nicht den Anforderungen;* she's just had her coming-out party: *sie ist gerade in die Gesellschaft eingeführt worden;* that's quite a comedown for him: *das ist ein arger Absturz für ihn;* now that I come to think of it: *wenn ich's recht bedenke.*

do:

It will do: *das wird genügen; das geht gerade;* I'll make

53

it do: *ich werde schon damit auskommen;* what's doing?: *was ist los?;* nothing doing!: *ausgeschlossen!; nichts zu machen!;* he's doing time: *er sitzt (seine Strafe ab);* he's done for: *er ist erledigt;* what can I do for you?: *was kann ich für Sie tun?; (Angestellter zum Kunden): womit kann ich (Ihnen) dienen?;* do without it!: *verzichte darauf!;* it's just not done: *das tut man einfach nicht;* after all is said and done: *schließlich und endlich;* may I? please do!: *darf ich? bitte schön!;* I like mine well-done: *für mich gut durchgebraten;* that'll be his undoing: *das wird sein Verderben sein.*

go:

Let's go Dutch!: *jeder zahlt für sich selbst;* nice going!: *gut gemacht!;* let's go native!: *zurück zur Natur!;* let's go places!: *gehen wir bummeln!;* it's a go!: *topp!, abgemacht!;* let's have a go at it: *versuchen wir's mal;* he's always on the go: *er hat kein Sitzfleisch, er ist immer auf dem Sprung;* a go-between: *ein Vermittler;* he's a goner: *er ist erledigt, er ist ein toter Mann;* there were wild goings-on: *es ging toll her;* going! going! gone!: *zum ersten! zum zweiten! zum dritten (Mal)!;* they're going steady: *sie gehen miteinander;* she is going steady: *sie ist in festen Händen;* and that goes for you, too!: *das gilt auch für Sie!*

run:

Feeling ran high: *die Wogen der Erregung gingen hoch;* running board: *Trittbrett;* two days running: *zwei Tage hintereinander;* he had a running nose: *seine Nase lief;* running stitch: *Stilstich;* a running start: *ein fliegender*

54

Start; the play had a long run: *das Stück hatte viele en suite-Vorstellungen* (or *fortlaufende Wiederholungen*); he had the run of the place: *die Räumlichkeiten standen ganz zu seiner Verfügung;* they gave me the run-around: *sie haben mich von Pontius zu Pilatus geschickt;* I had a run-in with the police: *ich hatte ein Renkontre mit der Polizei;* I'm run down: *ich bin ganz herunter.*

keep:

He keeps to himself: *er sondert sich ab, er lebt für sich;* keep at it!: *laß nicht locker!;* let's play for keeps: *spielen wir im Ernst;* that's not quite in keeping with his position: *das steht nicht ganz in Einklang mit seiner Stellung;* she is a kept woman: *sie läßt sich aushalten.*

take:

Can't you take a joke?: *verstehen Sie denn gar keinen Spaß?;* he can take it: *er kann einen Puff aushalten;* I take it that . . . : *ich nehme an, daß . . . ;* take a letter!: *schreiben Sie, bitte!;* I'll take you up on that: *ich nehme dich beim Wort;* take it from me: *laß es dir von mir gesagt sein;* we're about to take off: *wir werden gleich abfliegen;* she took him off well: *sie imitierte ihn gut.*

up:

put up:

He puts up a big front: *es ist vieles nur Fassade bei ihm;* they put up a good fight: *sie haben sich tapfer gehalten;* let's put it up to an impartial observer: *überlassen wir die Entscheidung einem Unparteiischen!;* who put you up to it?: *wer hat dich darauf gebracht?;* put 'em up!: *Hände hoch!;*

can you put me up?: *können Sie mich unterbringen?;* he puts up with everything: *er läßt sich alles gefallen;* he puts up with it: *er gibt sich damit zufrieden;* I have to put up with much: *ich muß viel einstecken;* put up or shut up!: *Beweise her oder Maul halten!;* it was a put-up job: *es war ein abgekartetes Spiel.*

*up+*verb, used as noun:

The candidate was given a build-up: *der Kandidat wurde groß herausgestellt;* a thorough checkup was made of the criminals: *die Verbrecher wurden genau unter die Lupe genommen;* after the crackup a close-up was taken: *nach dem Zusammenstoß wurde eine Großaufnahme gemacht;* there was a shake-up among the higher-ups: *es wurden bei den höheren Stellen Veränderungen vorgenommen;* there's no let-up in our work: *unsere Arbeit läßt nicht nach;* there was a mix-up in the line-up: *in der Aufstellung gab es ein Durcheinander;* the pick-up, although without make-up, was stuck-up: *die Straßenbekanntschaft, obgleich ungepudert und ungeschminkt, war hochnäsig;* it's a toss-up between the two: *es kann ebenso gut der eine wie der andere sein;* a holdup: *ein Raubanfall;* a runner-up: *Zweiter;* math make-ups: *Nachprüfungen in Mathematik;* the setup: *die Anordnung;* a slip-up: *ein kleiner Fehler, ein Versehen;* smash-up: *Zusammenstoß;* a bad write-up: *eine schlechte Kritik;* a tie-up: *eine Verkehrsstörung; Stockung.*

up as adverb:

What's up?: *was geht hier vor?;* who's up?: *wer ist an der Reihe?;* something's up: *es liegt etwas in der Luft;* the jig's up: *das Spiel ist aus;* he's up in the air: *er lebt auf de Mond;* up in arms: *in Waffen;* (*fig.*) *in Harnisch, empört;* v is up to no good: *er führt nichts Gutes im Schilde;* what ha 't you been up to?: *was hast du nun angestellt?;* you don know what I am up against: *du weißt nicht, wogegen ich anzukämpfen habe;* not up to snuff: *nicht ganz auf der Höhe;* that's right up my alley: *das ist gerade in meinem Fahrwasser;* it's up to him: *das hängt von ihm ab; es ist an ihm;* he's up against it: *er ist in einer Klemme; er hat dagegen anzukämpfen.*

Also: upstart: *Emporkömmling;* the ups and downs of life: *die Wechselfälle des Lebens;* up-to-the-minute news: *allerletze Nachrichten;* pent-up emotions: *aufgestaute Gefühle;* be quick on the uptake: *schnell kapieren;* setting-up excercises: *Freiübungen;* he's on the up and up: *er ist grundehrlich;* he's an up-and-coming young man: *der Junge berechtigt zu den besten Hoffnungen.*

off:

We were laid off: *wir wurden abgebaut;* read it off!: *lesen Sie es ab!;* she took him off: *sie kopierte ihn;* we saw her off (to the ship, train): *wir begleiteten sie (zum Schiff, Zug);* he's a little off: *bei ihm ist eine Schraube locker;* you're way off!: *du irrst dich um vieles;* (*fig.*) *da irrst du groß!;* my day off: *mein freier Tag;* this is an off-day for me: *heute geht mir alles schief;* an off-color joke: *ein verfänglicher Witz;* off-hand: *aus dem Stegreif;* off-stage: *hinter den Kulissen; nicht auf der Bühne;* I'm off booze: *ich rühre keine Alkohol mehr an;* right off the bat: *auf Anhieb;* off and on: *ab und zu;* he gave him the shirt off his back: *er gab ihm sein letztes Hemd;* he's living off the fat of the land: *er lebt herrlich und in Freuden;* he's well-off: *es geht ihm finanziell gut, er ist gut daran;* a cooling-off period: *eine Abkühlungsperiode;* that's the pay-off: *das schlägt dem Faß den Boden aus; das bringt das Ergebnis zu Tage.*

Such quick-change artists as the above English words, which can be made to play four or five syntactical roles in the sentence, are uncommon in German. In German, words can be more easily compounded and combined into noun-clusters but, as a rule, they retain their original function as noun, verb, etc. On the other hand, however, the English-speaking student meets with many difficulties in the various uses of the modal auxiliaries: **wollen, lassen, dürfen, mögen, müssen, sollen** and **können.**

wollen: *es will nicht gehen:* it won't go; *sie will morgen abreisen:* she intends to leave tomorrow; *er will es gesehen haben:* he claims he saw it; *das will ich meinen:* I should say so; *das will getan sein:* it's got to be done; *das will nicht viel sagen:* that doesn't mean much; *ich wollte es tun:* I meant to do it; *du hast gar nichts zu wollen:* you have no say in the matter; *ich wollte eben weggehen:* I was just about to leave; *das will ein Mann sein?:* do you call that a man?

lassen: *sie läßt sich nichts abgehen:* she denies herself nothing; *ich lasse Herrn N. bitten:* please show Mr. N. in; *das läßt tief blicken:* that gives you a deep insight, that tells a tale; *man muß es ihm lassen:* you've got to hand it to him; *er läßt sich nicht lumpen:* money's no object to him; *er läßt den lieben Gott einen guten Mann sein:* he lets things slide; *die Katze läßt das Mausen nicht:* the leopard won't change his spots; *das läßt sich hören:* (*das klingt recht und billig*) that sounds reasonable; (*jetzt haben Sie's getroffen!*): now you're talking!; *er läßt sich nichts sagen:* you can't tell him a thing; *er ließ sie in der Tinte:* he left her holding the bag; *er ließ sie aufsitzen:* he stood her up; *laß doch!:* don't bother!; *ich lasse ihn grüßen:* remember me to him; *er läßt sich kein X für ein U vormachen:* you can't put anything over on him; *er läßt mit sich reden:* he is open to reason; he will compromise; *er ließ nichts unversucht:* he left no stone unturned; *das lasse ich mir nicht einreden:* I won't be talked into it; *lassen Sie das Spaßen!:* stop joking!; *ich lasse mir ein Haus bauen:* I'm having a house built; *er läßt sich die Haare schneiden:* he is having his hair cut; *das läßt sich denken:* that can be imagined; *es läßt sich nicht leugnen:* it cannot be denied; *ich ließ es hingehen:* I let it pass; *ich lasse ihn fallen:* I won't support him any longer; *dagegen läßt sich nichts einwenden:* there are no objections to it; *daran ließ sich nicht zweifeln:* you couldn't doubt it; *ich lass' mir nicht gern befehlen:* I don't like to be ordered about; *ich lasse mich nicht einschüchtern:* I'll not (let myself) be browbeaten; *er läßt mich die ganze schwere Arbeit allein machen:* he has me do all the hard work alone.

dürfen: *wenn ich so sagen darf:* if I may express myself in this manner; *Sie dürfen nicht hingehen:* you mustn't go there; *man darf dabei nicht vergessen:* in this connection it should not be forgotten; *Sie dürfen nur klingeln:* all you need do is ring; *das dürfte der Fall sein:* that might well be so; *wie darfst du mir das antun?:* how can you do such a thing to me?; *eigentlich dürfte ich dir ja nicht verzeihen:* I really shouldn't forgive you; *Sie dürfen auch wohl einmal zu uns kommen:* why don't you come to see us once in a while?; *wenn ich bitten darf:* (if you) please!; *darf ich Sie um den nächsten Tanz bitten?* may I have the next dance?; *er bat, sich zurückziehen zu dürfen:* he asked to be allowed to withdraw; *es dürfte sich wohl um einen Irrtum handeln:* it is probably just a mistake; *wir dürfen es bezweifeln:* we have reason to doubt it.

mögen: *das mag wohl sein:* that may very well be; *mag er fortgehen oder bleiben:* whether he go or stay; *was ich auch immer tun mag:* whatever I might do; *mag es tun, wer es kann:* let anybody do it who can; *mag sie auch noch so schön sein:* may she be ever so beautiful; *was mag er sich wohl gedacht haben:* what may he have imagined?; *wer mag es ihm gesagt haben?:* I wonder who told him; *das möchte nicht ganz leicht sein:* I'm afraid it's not so easy; *ich möchte beinahe weglaufen:* I've half a mind to run off; *sage ihm, er möge gehen:* tell him to go; *er dachte nach, was das Wort wohl bedeuten möge:* he wondered what the word could possibly mean; *die beiden mögen sich:* the two are fond of each other; *mögen die Leute sagen, was sie wollen:* let people say what they wish; *so reich er auch sein mag:* however rich he may be; *er mag sich nur in Acht nehmen!:* he had better take care; *sagen Sie ihm, er möchte uns abholen:* tell him to call for us (or: to pick us up); *ich wünschte, er möchte kommen:* I wish he would come; *ich fürchtete, er möchte sich blamieren:* I was afraid he would put his foot into it.

müssen: *er muß bald hier sein:* he's due to be here soon;

ich mußte lachen: I couldn't help laughing; *das mußte nun einmal so sein:* fate would just have it so; *gerade ihn mußte ich treffen:* I had to meet him, of all people; *er mußte mir gerade jetzt in den Weg laufen:* of all times, he had to run into me now; *da muß auch noch das Auto kaputt gehen:* then also the auto has to go and break down; *du müßtest bei deiner vielen Arbeit schon steinreich sein:* you should be awfully rich by now considering the work you've put in; *er muß wohl abfällig über ihn geurteilt haben:* he must have judged him unfavorably; *Sie müssen wissen:* you should know; *das müßte noch heute geschehen:* that ought to be done by today; *er hätte schneller fahren müssen:* he should have driven faster; *sie müßte bald kommen:* she is bound to come soon; *er hat es tun müssen:* he had to do it; *er muß es getan haben:* he must have done it.

sollen: *du sollst das tun:* you should do that; *er soll mal eben ans Telephon kommen:* tell him he's wanted on the phone; *bald darnach sollte er abreisen:* he was expected to depart soon thereafter; *wie sollte er das wissen?:* how could he be expected to know that?; *soll das ein Scherz sein?:* do you call that a joke?; *was soll das?:* what's the point of that?; *wen anders sollte ich treffen als ....:* whom should I meet but . . . ; *wie soll man da ernst bleiben?:* how can one be serious in such a case?; *man sollte glauben:* one would imagine; *mit diesen Leuten soll man etwas fertig kriegen!:* how can you get anything done with people like that?; *wenn ich teilnehmen soll . . . . :* if I am to take part . . . ; *er soll das Buch gestohlen haben:* he is said to have stolen the book; *er hat kommen sollen:* he was expected to come; *er* *hätte das lesen sollen:* he ought to have read it; *eine Frau wie sie sein soll:* a model woman.

können: *ich kann schwimmen:* I can swim; *ich kann Deutsch:* I know German; *kann ich ihn sprechen?:* may I see him?; *wer kann das sein?:* who can that be?; *ich kann nicht mehr:* I can't go on any longer; *er lief, was er konnte:* he ran his hardest; *er hat es tun können:* he was able to do it; *er kann es getan haben:* he may have done it.

Modal auxiliaries often occur together in the same sentence:
Man soll nicht einmal reden dürfen?: aren't we even allowed to talk?; *er hätte das dürfen sollen:* he should have been allowed to do it; *er wird wohl wollen müssen:* he'll just have to want to; *ich glaube, das sein lassen zu dürfen:* I believe I can afford to let it go; *sie werden verzichten lernen müssen:* they will have to learn how to do without.

IV. EXPLETIVES

The function of the small words *zwar, wohl, schon, erst, doch, ja, auch, mal* and *nur* (which are known as *Flickwörter,* expletives or patchwords) is diametrically opposed to that performed by the overworked verbal drudges considered in the last chapter. These airy particles are not chained to any given grammatical category and are unencumbered by case, number or gender. This isolates them from their fellow-members and from the central configuration of the sentence structure. These nude, innocent words, however, answer a deep human need. They come to us from the distant cradle of living speech and silently invade the dead realm of written language, adding the human touch to the drab, closed sentence. It is part of man's revolt against the rigid laws of language in his struggle to wrest from it its refractory truths.

The student is at first inclined to overlook these inconspicuous particles. But they soon prove troublesome, for they represent delicate distinctions difficult to render into other languages. In English we rely more on stress and intonation, depending on the context, to indicate the slight but decisive manner in which these *Flickwörter* affect the sentence.

zwar:

Zwar ist es schon lange her: it is a long time ago, to be sure; *ich bin zwar der Vater:* I am, it is true, his father; *das ist zwar nicht gerade schön, aber nützlich:* this may not be exactly nice, but it is useful; *er ist ein Bösewicht, und zwar von der gefährlichsten Art:* he is a villain, and a most

63

dangerous one at that; *ich habe schon geschrieben, und zwar recht ausführlich:* I've already written and, what is more, quite explicitly; *sie haben ein Kind, und zwar einen Sohn:* they have one child, and that happens to be a son; *er ist zwar gescheit, aber . . . :* he is clever, I grant, but . . . ; *er kam zwar, doch war's zu spät:* he came all right, but too late; *sie spielt zwar Klavier, ist aber keine Künstlerin:* yes, she plays the piano; she's no artist, though; *zwar weiß ich viel, doch möchte ich mehr wissen:* much as I know, I wish I knew more.

wohl:

Er wird wohl kommen: I expect he'll come; *würden Sie mir wohl sagen:* I wonder if you would tell me; *wohl wahr, aber . . :* quite true, but . . . ; *dies ist wohl Dr. N.:* Dr. N., I presume; *Sie irren sich wohl:* I'm afraid you're wrong; *ich verstehe mich wohl selbst nicht:* very likely I fail to understand myself; *das habe ich mir wohl gedacht:* I thought as much; *ob er mich wohl noch kennt:* I wonder whether he still knows me; *es sind wohl drei Jahre:* I should say it's about three years; *er kommt wohl heute:* I suppose he'll come today; *das mag wohl sein:* that may very well be; *das ist wohl nicht möglich:* that's hardly possible; *ich weiß wohl, daß . . . :* I am perfectly aware of the fact that . . . ; *das wird wohl ganz richtig sein:* I dare say it is quite true; *aber er hütete sich wohl, davon zu sprechen:* he was careful, though, not to speak about it; *er ist wohl ein angesehener Mann, aber . . . :* no doubt he is a man of consequence, but . . . ; *wer ist das wohl?:* who on earth may that be?; *verstehen Sie (mich) wohl:* please get me right; *es gibt wohl Leute, die* . . . 1. (*es gibt vermutlich Leute, die* . . .) I suppose there are people who . . . ; 2. (*es gibt zwar Leute, die* . . .) there may be people who . . . ; it is true (I admit) there are people . . .

schon:

Es wird schon gehen: that'll go off all right; *Sie haben schon Recht, aber* . . . ; you're quite right, but . . . ; *schon der Gedanke:* the very idea; *schon im Herbst 1939:* as early as the autumn of 1939; *schon am frühen Morgen:* as soon as the day broke; *schon am nächsten Tag:* the very next day; *schon höchste Zeit:* it's high time; *schon erledigt!:* well, that's settled!; *was ist schon dabei?:* what of it!; *und wenn schon?:* so what!; *wer glaubt das schon?:* who on earth would believe it?; *wenn schon, denn schon:* let's go the whole hog; *was ist denn schon wieder (los)?:* what's the matter now?; *schon weil er blind ist* . . . : for the very reason that he is blind . . . ; *es wird sich schon finden:* it'll come out all right in the end; *ich werde ihn schon bezahlen:* I'll pay him all right; *schon gut:* 1. (*es ist schon in Ordnung*) that's all right that'll do; 2. (*schon richtig, aber* . . .) that's all very well, but . . . ; 3. (*das sagen Sie nur so*) you're just talking; *ich gebe schon zu, daß* . . . : I'm willing to admit that . . ; *das ist schon ganz richtig, aber* . . . : that's all very true, but . . . ; *ja, das kennen wir schon:* well, that's an old story; *schon der Name:* the bare name; *schon der Höflichkeit halber:* out of sheer politeness; *Sie werden mich schon verstehen:* I'm sure you'll understand me; *ich werde es schon machen:* I'll do it, I assure you; *er hat's schon wieder getan:* he's gone and done it again.

erst:

Wenn ich erst in Paris bin . . . ; once I'm in Paris . . . ;
es muß sich erst noch zeigen: that remains to be seen; *das
macht's erst recht schlimm:* that makes it all the worse; *nun
tu ich's erst recht nicht!:* now I certainly won't!; *er kam
erst, als . . . :* he did not come until . . . ; *erst vor drei
Tagen . . . :* only three days ago . . . ; *erst gestern erfuhr
ich es:* I got to know about it only yesterday; *ich habe erst
zehn Seiten gelesen:* I have read only ten pages so far; *erst
gehen, dann laufen:* before you can run you must learn to
walk; *erst das Geschäft, und dann das Vergnügen:* business
before pleasure; *für ihn muß eine Frau erst noch geboren
werden:* the woman he'll marry hasn't been born yet; *das
muß erst noch erfunden werden:* that has still to be invented
(and I doubt it ever will).

doch:

Sagen Sie es ihm doch: why don't you go and tell him?;
zeigen Sie es mir doch mal: show it to me, will you?; *ich
brauche doch keine Angst zu haben:* I surely don't have to
be afraid; *doch, ich sehe es:* yes, I do see it; *doch!:* of
course! (in refutation of an assumed premise); *Sie wissen
doch, daß . . . !:* You must surely know that . . . ; *was doch der
Grund sein mag!:* I wonder what the reason may be!; *das
ist doch zu arg:* that's really too bad; *das kann dem doch
nichts schaden:* come, come, that won't hurt him; *kommen
Sie doch herein!:* do come in!; *sei doch geduldig!:* now, be
patient!; *laß (es) doch!:* forget it!, skip it!; *das ist doch nicht
möglich:* that isn't really possible; *er war doch immerhin ein
guter Arbeiter:* he was a good worker, say what you will;

er hat also doch vergessen: so he forgot after all; *es paßt mir zwar nicht, aber ich werde es doch tun:* I don't like it but I'll do it all the same; *wenn es doch dunkler wäre!:* if it were only darker! *Er ist nicht gekommen. Doch!:* he hasn't come. Yes, he has. *Er ist doch nicht krank?:* don't tell me he's sick; *Sie kommen doch?:* you'll come, won't you?

ja:

Ja, doch!: of course; *daß du dich nur ja nicht erkältest!:* now, don't go and catch cold!; *daß du dich ja warm hältst!:* mind you, keep warm!; *ja, selbst der König . . :* nay, even the king . . . ; *Hunderte, ja Tausende:* hundreds, nay thousands; *das ist ja gar nicht schwer:* that's not hard at all; *das schadet ja gar nichts:* it doesn't matter, you see; *da sind Sie ja endlich:* there you are at last; *ich habe es dir ja gesagt:* I told you, didn't I?; *ja, was ich sagen wollte:* oh, by the way; *ja, das ist was anderes:* come now, that's different; *er war ja der Chef:* he was, after all, the boss; *es ist ja lächerlich:* it is really ridiculous; *ich kann ja nichts dafür:* I'm not really responsible for it; *er konnte nicht schwimmen, ich ja:* he didn't know how to swim; I did; *habe ich recht, ja?:* I'm right, am I not?; *ja, also eigentlich . . . :* well, actually . . . ; *aber ja!:* naturally!; *das ist ja fürchterlich!:* why, that's outrageous!; *kommen Sie ja rechtzeitig!:* be sure to come on time!; *tun Sie das ja nicht!:* for goodness' sake, don't do it!

auch:

Ich gehe mit.—Ich auch: I'm going along.—So am I. *Ich bleibe nicht länger hier.—Ich auch nicht:* I am not staying here any longer.—Nor am I. *Auch die besten Lehrer:* even the best teachers; *wo er auch sein mag:* wherever he may be. *Du siehst krank aus.—Ich b i n auch krank:* You look ill.— I *am* ill. *Ich darf auch nicht vergessen:* I also mustn't forget; *er war erfolgreich; er hat auch schwer gearbeitet:* he was successful but he did work hard enough, (don't you think?); *das will ich auch tun:* I intend to do just that; *wozu denn auch?:* why should I (you, he etc.)?

mal:

Laß mal sehen!: just let me have a look!; *erlauben Sie mal!* 1. (polite request:) if you please, permit me; 2. (protest:) well, I must say!; *es ist nun mal so:* that's the way things are; *es ist mal nicht anders:* such is life.

nur:

Wie kann man nur so empfindlich sein?: how can one be so touchy?; *wenn er nur schon käme!:* if he were only here!; *wenn der Krieg nur schon (mal) zu Ende wäre:* if the war were only over!; *er spielt nur:* he's only toying; *nur dies nicht!:* anything but that!; *er mag nur gehen:* let him go if he wants to; *warte nur!:* just wait!; *tue es nur ja nicht!:* please, don't do it!; *wie kam er nur hierher!:* how on earth did he get here!; *soviel ich nur kann:* as much as I can; *das beste, was man sich nur denken kann:* the best one could possibly imagine.

V. USEFUL EXPRESSIONS, CHIEFLY VITUPERATIVE

A good part of our lives is spent in altercation, wrangling, bickering, squabbles and brawls. Hardly an hour passes without vexations and petty annoyances of one kind or another. Mere vicinity is sufficient provocation for dispute. Nor is this distressing trait in our character absent from refined and educated circles, which are particularly self-assertive, opinionated and irritable. The sentiment of love assuages but does not banish this imperfection in our nature. Indeed, contentiousness rankles in the very bosom of family life where the warm atmosphere of intimacy renders it more poignant. It seems we were not made to live in peace with one another. Fortunately, the fear of retaliation mollifies the asperity of this alarming propensity and blows give way to abusive language and tongue-lashing.

The Germans are not totally unacquainted with these ugly passions, which trickle down the foul cavern of the human heart. Indeed, a hankering after altercation, prompted by a spirit of contradiction and disdain of intellectual compromise, is a prominent ingredient in the mental make-up of the Germans. Their language, therefore, abounds in strong, baleful words, cantankerous phrases and unseemly interjections which are repeated with perseverance and conviction. Such retentive virtue resides in them that they make us redden and jump, and often threaten to throw us into confusion. Our reaction to such language is direct and instantaneous. Although lightly negotiated on the tongue, these phrases sear the flesh and penetrate to the bone. Their fatal sound alone sets violent passions in motion.

This is a gloomy subject and only the devil can take delight in it. But it would be unfair to deprive the eager student of such a fertile area of linguistic activity not found in textbooks. To have rancor in one's heart and no ready word on one's tongue is one of the most exasperating experiences of a foreigner. The student, however, is cautioned to use these verbal indelicacies sparingly, for they may not always be *salonfähig* (acceptable in good society, fit for innocent ears) and under certain conditions may even be *verpönt* (taboo). He would also do well to take into consideration the sex, size and social position of his listeners. The *Reibungsflächen* (areas of friction) in which Germans may discharge their emotions in conventionalized phrases fall under the following headings:

Zurücksetzungen (slights, rebuffs), *Rechthaberei* (self-righteous dogmatism), *Kasernenhofton* (drill-ground blustering), *Anschnauzen* (the abusive language of bullying), *Sekkieren* (bother, annoyances), *Derbheiten* (coarse humor), *Schikane* (paltry, annoying trick(s)), *Kaschemmentonausdrücke* (foul language of the tavern), *herausfordernde Haltung* (chip-on-the-shoulder attitude), *Sticheleien* (cutting remarks, gibes), *Grobheiten* (affronts, coarse remarks), *Ehrverletzungen* (smears, slander), *Anrempelungen* (attacks in a vulgar manner), *Ulk* (practical jokes, banter), *Anmaßungen* (overbearing insolence), *Verächtlichmachung* (disparagement, pooh-poohing), *necken, hänseln, frotzeln, verkohlen, veräppeln, aufziehen, verhohnepipeln*, (tease, razz, josh, kid mock, make one the butt of jokes, taunt), *Krachschlagen* (kick up a row), *Krawall* (bang-up affair), *Radau* (rough-house).

Was fällt Ihnen denn ein?: what's the big idea?; *aber was denn!:* come, come!; *so schaust du aus!:* who, you? are you the man to do that?; *wissen Sie, mit wem Sie es zu tun haben?:* who do you think you're talking to?; *was ist in dich gefahren?:* what's gotten into you?; *wie gefällt dir das!:* how do you like that!; *hat man je so was erlebt?:* did you ever see the likes of it?; *du hast die richtige Revolver-schnauze!:* stop shooting off your big mouth!; *du kannst mir den Buckel runterrutschen!:* jump in the lake!, go sit on a tack!; *du kannst Gift darauf nehmen:* you can bet your bottom dollar; *ich habe ihm die Leviten gelesen:* I told him where to get off; *aus dir wird kein Schwein klug:* I can't make you out for the life of me; *du bist unausstehlich!:* you're a pain in the neck!; *du hast einen gehörigen Bock geschossen:* you sure pulled a boner; *du hast das Pulver nicht erfunden:* you won't set the world on fire; *er glaubt, er hört das Gras wachsen:* he thinks he's the cat's whiskers; *Sie haben gut reden:* it is easy for you to talk; talk is cheap; *das geht dich einen Dreck an:* that's none of your darn business; *er blies ihr den Marsch:* he gave her a piece of his mind; *du bist ein Pechvogel!:* you've got the jinx; *er nimmt sich kein Blatt vor den Mund:* he makes no bones about it; *du bist ein großer Schwindelmeier:* you're a gyp artist; *ich werde ihm schon sagen, was die Glocke geschlagen hat!:* I'll tell him where to get off with that stuff; *damit ist's Essig!:* no soap! nothing doing!; *da schlägt's dreizehn:* that's the pay-off!; *ausgerechnet jetzt!*: now, of all times!; *der Groschen ist gefallen!*: it's finally dawned on him; now he gets the point of the joke; *geh nicht wie die Katz um den heißen Brei!*: stop beating around the bush!; *du bist nicht sehr schlagfertig!*: you're not very quick on the trigger; *du hast eine lange Leitung!*: you're not very fast on the uptake!; *man muß es dir mit dem Nürnberger Trichter eingeben*: it's got to be pounded into you; *sprich, wie dir der Schnabel gewachsen ist*: cut the highfalutin talk!; *sie hat ihn durch den Kakao gezogen*: she pulled his leg; *das Ei des Kolumbus*: elementary, my dear Watson!; *du hast Dreck am Stecken*: you have skeletons in your closet; *sie ging dir nicht auf den Leim*: she didn't fall for your line; *die Dummen werden nicht alle*: there's a sucker born every minute; *Alter schützt vor Torheit nicht*: there's no fool like an old fool; *sei keine gekränkte Leberwurst*: don't be a sorehead; *eine Laus ist ihm über die Leber gelaufen*: he's peeved; *ich kenne meine Pappenheimer*: how well I know them!; I've got their number; *drehst Du den Spieß um?*: are your turning the tables on me?; *so fragt man die Bauern aus!*: stop pumping me!; *ich fresse einen Besen, wenn . . .* : well, I'll eat my hat if . . . ; *ich habe ein Hühnchen mit Ihnen zu rupfen*: I've a bone to pick with you; *du hast keine Ahnung von Tuten und Blasen*: you know as much about it as the man in the moon; *du gönnst mir nicht das Weiße im Auge*: you begrudge me the shirt on my back; *hängen Sie es nicht an die große Glocke!*: you don't have to shout it from the housetops! *man muß die Kirche im Dorf lassen*: now, that's going too far!; *du hast das Mundwerk am rechten Fleck*: you know all the answers; *sie hat Haare auf den Zähnen:* she's a tough customer; *er läuft uns fast das Haus ein:* he won't take "no" for an answer; *der Hieb sitzt:* that struck home; *mach gute Miene zum bösen Spiel:* grin and bear it!; *ihm fehlt der gesunde Menschenverstand:* he needs a little horse sense; *er hat den Knigge wohl nicht gelesen?:* he hasn't read Emily Post?; *noch ist Polen nicht verloren:* down but not out; *so schnell schießen die Preußen nicht:* we are not that quick on the trigger; *es wird nicht so heiß gegessen wie gekocht:* things are never as bad as they seem; *darüber läßt sich streiten:* that's open to dispute; *es ist mir Jacke wie Hose:* I don't give a hoot one way or the other; *das ist der Gipfelpunkt!:* that beats everything; *er ist eine taube Nuß:* he's dead from the neck up; *die Sache hat einen Haken:* there's a catch to it; *damit kannst du dich begraben lassen!:* it's not worth a tinker's dam; *du gehst über Leichen:* you'll stop at nothing!; *du bist noch nicht trocken hinter den Ohren:* you're green as grass; *das ist so klar wie dicke Tinte:* that's as clear as mud; *da pfeift es aus einem anderen Loch:* that's a horse of another color; *er lügt, daß sich die Balken biegen:* he lies like a trooper; *so ein Bart!:* that story is as old as the hills; *du verstehst dich darauf wie ein Blinder auf die Farben:* you know as much about that as the man in the moon; *er ist ein Nassauer:* he's a sponger; *er hat Ellenbogen:* he's a pusher, he's aggressive; *ein Esel schimpft den anderen Langohr:* the pot calls the kettle black; *das Hemd ist mir näher als der Rock:* charity begins at home; *hin ist hin:* there's no use crying over spilt milk; *wer zuerst kommt, mahlt zuerst:* first come, first served; *wo nichts ist, hat der*

Kaiser sein Recht verloren: you can't squeeze blood out of a turnip; *ich glaube, mich laust der Affe:* well, I'll be . . . ; *ich lasse mich nicht so leicht unterkriegen:* I'll give 'em a run for their money; *hinterm Berge wohnen auch Leute:* you're not the only pebble on the beach; *hast Du eine Ahnung!:* you haven't the faintest idea; *sie muß wie ein rohes Ei behandelt werden:* you've got to treat her with kid gloves; *er tut, als könne er nicht bis drei zählen:* you'd think he couldn't say boo; *du gibst aber an!:* a) *(schneidest auf):* my, you're bragging; b) *(machst Aufhebens)* my, you're fussy; *sie schmierte ihm Honig ums Maul:* she soft-soaped him; *ein toter Hund beißt nicht:* dead men tell no tales; *sie ist eine dumme Gans:* she's a dumb Dora; *Pack schlägt sich, Pack verträgt sich:* cads' fighting when ended is very soon mended.

Although it is lawful to give vent to indignation to repel injustice and to indulge in vituperative language when we ourselves are the object of ill-treatment, it is unwise to become habituated to strong language unless reparation cannot otherwise be obtained, for the subsequent inward uneasiness and attendant remorse is disproportionate to the extent of the injury. It is a deplorable circumstance that occasions which give rise to mirth are less frequent than those which cause vexation. Yet few of us are wholly given over to resentment and no man sinks so low as to relinquish his claims on courtesy. For that very reason, therefore, artificial tenderness (compliments, greetings, circumlocutions, ingratiating remarks, small talk about the weather, etc.) should be cultivated with relish. The practice of such forms of courtesy dispels petulancy, improves the temper and restores tranquility of spirit. It would, therefore, be an unpardonable negligence (and a mortal blow to chivalry) to withhold from the student models of polite conversation and soft answers designed to mollify, if not obliterate, the natural turbulency of our natures:

EVASIVE ANSWERS (*Ausweichende Antworten*):

Ich habe darüber keine Meinung: I have no independent opinion on the subject; *es ist mehr oder weniger Geschmacksache:* it is more or less a matter of taste; *nicht daß ich wüßte:* not that I know of; *es scheint so:* it looks that way; *mag sein:* could be.

WEATHER:

Was halten Sie vom Wetter?: what does the weather look like to you?; *ich glaube, wir bekommen schönes Wetter:* I think we'll have nice weather; *hoffentlich bleibt's so:* I hope it stays like this; *es wird schön werden:* we'll have a fine day; *es gießt:* it's pouring; *es ist scheußlich:* horrible weather; *ein wahres Hundewetter:* beastly weather.

POLITE PHRASES:

Würden Sie so freundlich sein, mir zu sagen . . . : would you be good enough to tell me . . . ; *womit kann ich Ihnen dienen?:* what can I do for you?; *Sie wünschen?:* what can I do for you?; (waiter:) what's yours, please?; *wie erklärt sich's, daß . . . :* how do you account for the fact that . . . ; *was versteht man unter . . . :* what do you understand by . . . ; *darf ich die Herrschaften miteinander bekannt machen?:* may

I introduce you; *freut mich, Sie kennen zu lernen:* I'm delighted to meet you; *Verzeihung, ich habe nicht recht verstanden:* sorry, I didn't quite understand; *recht gerne!:* I'd be glad to; *meinen Sie nicht auch, daß . . . :* are you not also of the opinion that . . . . ; *gestatten Sie, ist dieser Platz frei?:* excuse me, is this seat taken?; *bedauere, dieser Platz ist besetzt:* sorry, the seat's occupied; *bitte, greifen Sie zu:* please help yourself!; *machen Sie meinetwegen keine Umstände:* don't trouble yourself on my account; *ich kann mich nicht beklagen:* I can't complain; *wie werden Sie das auf Deutsch wiedergeben?:* how would you render that in German?; *ich wäre Ihnen sehr verbunden:* I'd be much obliged; *jetzt muß ich mich verabschieden:* I've got to leave now; *schönen Gruß zu Hause:* regards to the folks; *empfehlen Sie mich Ihren Eltern:* give my regards to your parents; *ich werde es gern ausrichten:* I'll be happy to convey the message.

VI. IDIOMS, QUOTATIONS, PROVERBS, SAYINGS

The German language abounds in idioms (*spracheigene Redensarten*) which impart to the language originality and the native touch. Besides, however, there are plenty of proverbs (*Sprichwörter*), sayings (*Aussprüche*), quotations (*Zitate*), maxims (*Sentenzen*), aphorisms (*Gedankensplitter*), slogans and catch-phrases (*Schlagworte*), quips (*Witzworte*) and stale puns (*Kalauer*), which easily degenerate into ready-made clichés and hackneyed phrases (*abgedroschene Redensarten*), the frequent use of which shows bad taste and is a sure sign of an intellectual prig (*Bildungsphilister*). Yet, a judicious use of such phrases cannot be condemned. A set phrase thrown in at the proper moment, a quotation used not to adorn inferior matter but to touch a chord of association may often save a lagging conversation from boredom.

SOME WELL-WORN QUOTATIONS:

Spät kommt er, doch er kommt: He's late but he's coming after all. (*Schiller, Wallenstein*).

Ich kenne meine Pappenheimer: I know my Pappenheimers, i.e. my trusted soldiers of the Pappenheim regiment; meaning: I know my customers, I know whom I'm dealing with. (*Schiller, Wallenstein*).

Gut gebrüllt, Löwe!: Well roared, lion! (Shakespeare, Midsummer Night's Dream).

Der Mohr hat seine Schuldigkeit getan, der Mohr kann

77

gehen: The Moor has done his duty, the Moor's dismissed. (*Schiller, Fiesco*).

Du sprichst ein großes Wort gelassen aus: You utter a great word with unconcern; often humorously meaning: You've said quite a mouthful. (*Goethe, Iphigenie*).

Spiegelberg, ich kenne dich!: Spiegelberg, I know you; meaning: I've got your number. (*Schiller, Räuber*).

Noch ist Polen nicht verloren: Poland is not lost yet; meaning: Down but not out. (Polish folk song).

Erlaubt ist, was gefällt: All is permitted that pleases. (*Goethe, Tasso*).

Kein Mensch muß müssen: There's no such thing as must. (*Lessing, Nathan der Weise*).

Unfortunately, people, in an ill-advised humorous mood, sometimes do not shrink from a blasphemous use of their most revered classics—and Germans are no exception:

Der Not gehorchend, nicht dem eigenen Triebe: Yielding to necessity, not to an impulse of our own; facetiously meaning: If you've got to go, you've got to go. (*Schiller, Braut von Messina*).

And if one should be moved to give vent to an unutterable vulgarity, he refers to *Goethe: Götz von Berlichingen,* Act III, Scene 4—commonly known as *Götz-Zitat.*

MISCELLANEOUS PHRASES AND PROVERBS:

Einem geschenkten Gaul sieht man nicht ins Maul: Don't look a gift horse in the mouth.

Ruhe ist die erste Bürgerpflicht: Peace and quiet is the

burgher's foremost duty; humorously meaning: Take it easy.

Wie du mir, so ich dir: I give you tit for tat.

Der Mensch denkt und Gott lenkt: Man proposes, God disposes.

Das Bessere ist des Guten Feind: The better is the enemy of the good.

Gedanken sind zollfrei: Thoughts are duty-free.

Dem Glücklichen schlägt keine Stunde: The hours do not strike for the happy man.

Mit der Dummheit kämpfen Götter selbst vergebens: Against stupidity the gods themselves struggle in vain.

Es ist dafür gesorgt, daß die Bäume nicht in den Himmel wachsen: There is a limit to all things.

Dem Blinden hilft keine Brille: A blind man won't thank you for a looking glass.

Vorsicht ist die Mutter der Weisheit: An ounce of prevention is worth a pound of cure.

PHRASES WHOSE IMAGERY IS NO LONGER FELT:

Auf die lange Bank schieben: Let things slide, drag out.

Mit einem blauen Auge davonkommen: Get off cheaply.

Das Blaue von Himmel lügen: Lie to beat the band.

Mal den Teufel nicht an die Wand!: Talk of the devil, and he will appear.

Er ist nicht auf den Mund gefallen: He has a ready tongue.

Wir machten uns aus dem Staube: We made off.

Sie sind verduftet: They disappeared into thin air.

Sie hat Haare auf den Zähnen: She knows all the answers.

Er gibt seinen Senf dazu: He puts in his two cents.

Eine Laus ist ihm über die Leber gelaufen: He's peeved.

Er spielt die gekränkte Leberwurst: He's a sorehead.

Er hat die Weisheit mit Löffeln gefressen: He makes a great show of learning.

Er lacht sich einen Ast: He's splitting his sides with laughter.

Er säuft wie ein Bürstenbinder: He drinks like a fish.

Der Himmel hängt ihm voller Geigen: He sees everything in a rosy light.

Wo gehobelt wird, fliegen Späne: You can't make an omelet without breaking eggs.

Da liegt der Hase im Pfeffer: That's the nigger in the woodpile.

Er ist bekannt wie ein bunter Hund: He is known all over town.

Er ist mit allen Hunden gehetzt: He is on to every dodge.

Da stehen die Ochsen am Berge, da steht man wie der Ochs am Berge: There you are at your wit's end.

VII. REGIONALISMS

Each region has its own inimitable dialect (*Mundart*), which is the familiar language of the home and the street. A dialect is not, as is often erroneously assumed, a corrupt form of High German. On the contrary, a standard written language (*einheitliche Schriftsprache*), loosely called High German (*Hochdeutsch*), is a late, artificial creation (*Kulturerzeugnis*) which did not come into being until the sixteenth century. Although the dialect is to be found in its purest form in the rustic speech of the peasant who speaks it naturally (*wie ihm der Schnabel gewachsen ist*), it is the real *Muttersprache* of all Germans, and was even spoken by Goethe and Schiller. This homely regional speech is not to be confused with special languages, such as student slang (*Studentensprache*) or the jargon of thieves (*Gaunersprache* or *Rotwelsch*) which serve primarily as a secret means of communication between a limited number of individuals of a particular group. High German (*Hochdeutsch* or *Schriftdeutsch*) is the common language (*Gemeinsprache*) of the educated classes, the radio and the press, and is spoken by the lower and middle classes with varying degrees of perfection. This *Gemeinsprache* itself, however, has no accepted uniform mode of speech (*Einheitssprache*), which exists only in the artificial standard speech of the stage (*Bühnensprache*). One can easily detect the native regional dialect of an educated German speaking High German, for it affects his vocabulary (*Wortschatz*), pronunciation (*Aussprache*), accent (*Betonung*) and mode of expression (*Ausdrucksweise*).

Among the bewildering varieties of German speech we may note only the following conspicuous differences:

The real Berliner (*der Berliner ist mit Spreewasser getauft*) is soon detected by his speech which, in the opinion of non-Berliners, is *vorlaut* (pert) and *schnodderig* (blustering). A Berliner talks a blue streak (*er hat die richtige Revolverschnauze*), is quick on the trigger (*schlagfertig*), doesn't pull his punches (*nimmt kein Blatt vor den Mund*) and cannot keep his trap shut (*er kann nicht das Maul halten*). Besides, the Berliner confuses *mir* and *mich*, says *ik* for *ich* and *det* for *das*. His inability to pronounce *g* is illustrated in the well-known, typical sentence: *eine gut gebratene Gans ist eine gute Gabe Gottes*—where every *g* is pronounced as a *y* (*eine jut jebratene Jans ist eine jute Jabe Jottes*).

The Swabian (*der Schwabe*) *schwäbelt* (speaks in the Swabian dialect). *Er ist im Schwabenalter* means "he has arrived at the age of forty" (which, for a Swabian, is the age of maturity); *ein Schwabenstreich* is a foolish action, a tomfoolery," as exemplified in the tale of *Die sieben Schwaben* (The seven Swabians).

The Saxonian (*der Sachse*) *sächselt*, which is generally regarded as a comical pronunciation. He pronounces the *k* as a *g*, and the *p* as a *b*.

The speech of the Rhinepfalz (Speyer, Landau) is recognized from afar by its loud, intense, unreserved nature, which gave rise to the designation of *Pfälzer Krischer* (*Kreischer*, means a "shrieker" or "screamer").

Niederdeutsch comprises those dialects spoken in north-west Germany that were unaffected by the High German sound shifts. *Pfund, Apfel, Affe, schlafen, Zeit, Wasser* are pronounced *pund, appel, ape, slapen, tid, water*—bringing it close to the English.

The South German dialects, on the other hand, (Austrian, Bavarian) have a broad pronunciation with variously broken or blended vowels, simple vowels often gliding into a vanish (*lieb* is pronounced *liab*, the *ia* forming a diphthong with stress on the *i* softly carrying over into a faint aftersound of *a*, similar to English "ear" in "fear"), diphthongs often blending into a uniform vowel (in Viennese, *Haus* is pronounced like English "hawss"), while the consonants conform more closely to those of High German and the written language than the consonants of the Berlin dialect. Austrians, except for a few special cases, never use the past tense of the indicative, replacing it by the present perfect (they say: *ich bin nach Hause gekommen,* rather than: *ich kam nach Hause*). On the whole, the Austrian dialects are considered softer and more *gemütlich* (genial) than their North German counterparts, corresponding to the happy-go-lucky disposition of the Austrian people.

VIII. SCHOOLS AND EDUCATION

A. In Germany

The cultural variations in the various *Länder* in Germany are reflected in the diversity of school systems. The necessity or desirability of the mutual adaptation of the different school systems is one of the most controversial questions in present-day Germany. These problems are dealt with by the "Standing Conference of Education Ministers," the "Cultural Political Committee of the Bundestag," the "Committee for German Education" (Federal Advisory Council), parent-teacher groups and various other municipal and economic organizations. In the Federal Republic of Germany the Land governments of the ten *Länder* (including West Berlin) are in charge of cultural affairs, just as they were before 1933, and are responsible for the organization and control of schools. In the Soviet Zone of Germany cultural affairs, as well as all other matters, are centrally controlled. All the German *Länder* provide for compulsory school attendance from the ages of 6 to 18 (Art. 145 of the Reich Constitution of Aug. 11, 1919; and Reich Law on Compulsory School Attendance of July 7, 1938). The minimum requirement is eight years full-time attendance (nine years in Berlin, Bremen, Hamburg, and Schleswig-Holstein) and two to three years of part-time vocational school (*Berufsschule*) with 4 to 12 study-hours per week during apprenticeship.

GENERAL SCHOOLS:

Between the ages of 3 and 5 the German child is sent

to a *Kleinkinderschule* (*Kindergarten* or *Kinderhort*) where he learns the elements of discipline and order. The child is then sent to a *Grundschule* (primary school) for 4 years (six years in Berlin, Bremen, Hamburg). Attendance is compulsory and the tuition is free. The schools are maintained by Government taxation. The primary school forms a part of the *Volksschule* (general school), in which about 80 per cent of all German children enroll after completing their primary schooling. There are separate *Volksschulen* for boys and girls, except in small towns where the schools are often coeducational. Generally, children of different religions (*Konfessionen*) are taught together (for which reason they are also called *Simultanschulen*), and religious instruction (*Religionsunterricht*) is imparted separately. In some of the smaller places, however, each religious group (*Glaubensgemeinschaft*) maintains its own *Volksschule*. The lowest class is called the first class, the next the second class, etc. (*erste Klasse, zweite*, etc.) until the eighth which is the final class. Instruction is given from 8 a.m. until 1 p.m. In the schools for boys the teachers are men, in those for girls the teachers are generally women.

Besides reading and writing, the chief courses of study (*Hauptfächer* or *Lehrgegenstände*) are arithmetic (*Rechnen*), geography (*Erdkunde, Heimatkunde*), science (*Naturkunde*), civics (*Bürgerkunde*), singing (*Singen*), drawing (*Zeichnen*), physical training (*Leibesübungen*), religion (*Religion*), fine arts, sewing, etc. (*Handfertigkeits- und Handarbeitsunterricht*) for girls only, and a foreign language (*Fremdsprache*) in the upper grades.

85

Teachers receive their training at training schools (*Pädagogische Akademien*). After passing a special examination (*Lehrerprüfung*) they begin to teach as *Schulamtsbewerber*, and then after two years take their second and final examination. In the larger schools the teachers (*Lehrkräfte*) are under the supervision of a *Rektor*. The *Volksschulen*, as all schools, are administered by the State, which maintains a Department of Education (*Kulturministerium*) for that purpose, with its subdivisions of the local *Kreisschulamt* and *Oberschulamt*, which supervise the schools, working in close conjunction with the individual communities.

Included in the *Volksschulen* are also the Special Schools (*Sonderschulen*) for the blind, the deaf, retarded and handicapped children. *Mittelschulen* or *Realschulen* are the *Volksschulen* which serve as preparatory schools for the professions. There are *Mittelschulen* with less exacting standards which do not lead to the University. Roughly 5 per cent of the school children go from the fourth grade (after passing an admission examination) to the *Mittelschule* or *Realschule*, where they study for six years (three years in Bavaria, where students transfer after the seventh grade of the general school). In these schools the students are prepared for business, home economics, technical and social occupations. About 15 per cent of the students (after passing entrance examinations) attend the *Höhere Schule*, which in a course of study lasting nine years prepares the student for the University or for careers in the civil service.

THE STANDARD SCHOOL:

The cities of Bremen, Hamburg, and Berlin have introduced what is known as the *Einheitsschule* (standard school or *Allgemeine Volksschule*), starting with a common six-year basic program and followed by a six-year advanced program divided into courses. In Hamburg and Berlin we find the "practical course" (three years full-time, three years part-time plus apprenticeship), the "technical course" (four years full-time, then part-time instruction), and the "academic course" (seven years full-time divided into several branches).

There are also private standard schools, such as the Waldorf School and the *Landerziehungsheime* (country boarding schools). Private Schools are defined as institutions not supported directly by the State, the community or any organization under public law.

SECONDARY EDUCATION:

Students who do not contemplate an academic career leave the *Volksschule* after eight years to engage in some trade or craft. The others leave after four years to attend a higher school of learning for nine years in preparation for the University. Girls go to a Lyceum. Boys may enter either a classical *Gymnasium* (which stresses Latin, Greek, and one modern foreign language), the *Realgymnasium* (which emphasizes Latin and two modern foreign languages), a *Reformrealgymnasium* (a nonclassical school with no Greek), a mathematics-science *Gymnasium* or *Oberrealschule* (which stresses mathematics, science, and modern languages). There are also mixed and special forms, such as *Auf-*

bauschulen (starting after the sixth or seventh grade of the general school), incomplete secondary schools (six-year program, no final examinations), and *Frauen-Oberschulen* (girls' schools which emphasize social studies and home economics). The *Gymnasien* consist of nine classes: Sexta, Quinta, Quarta, Untertertia, Obertertia, Untersekunda, Obersekunda, Unterprima, Oberprima. The upper classes are usually separated (*gegabelt*) into linguistic and scientific studies. At the end of the *Oberprima* the student takes his final examination (*das Abitur*), written and oral. If he passes the examination (*wenn er sie bestanden hat*) and has not failed (*nicht durchgefallen ist*), he receives his diploma (*Reifezeugnis*), which permits him to register (*immatrikulieren*) at a University or professional school (*Fachschule*).

VOCATIONAL SCHOOLS (*FACHSCHULEN*):

The *Fachschulen* are full-time, advanced vocational schools, covering almost all branches of industry and economy. Requirement for admission is the completion of apprenticeship or other vocational training. Full-time instruction is given lasting from four to eight semesters, depending on the vocational category or occupational level. The *Berufsschule* (part-time vocational school) offers part-time instruction during apprenticeship. It includes business, industrial, commercial, home economics, agricultural, and mining schools, as well as general vocational schools. The *Berufs-Fachschule* (full-time vocational school) requires for admission the completion of a *Volksschule* or Middle School program. It offers one, two, or more years of full-time vocational education, including courses in commerce, trade, foreign languages, home economics, etc. *Fachschulen* are generally of the following types: agricultural schools (*landwirtschaftliche Fachschulen—Landbau, Gärtnerei, Forstwesen*), business schools (*kaufmännische Fachschulen—Handelsschulen, Wirtschaft*), technical schools (*technische Fachschulen — Baugewerkschulen, Metallfach, Textilfach, Handwerk*), mining (*Bergschulen*), schools of navigation (*Seefahrtsschulen—Schiffsingenieur- und Seemaschinistenschulen*), home economics, nursing, domestic science for girls (*Frauenfachschulen—Haushaltungsschulen, Kinderpflege, Haushaltgehilfinnen, etc.*).

UNIVERSITIES (*HOCHSCHULEN*):

German universities are State institutions which require a *Reifezeugnis* of a *höhere Schule* for entrance. A student without such a *Reifezeugnis* may be an auditor (*Gasthörer*) at lectures (*Vorlesungen*) but may not sit for examinations (*Prüfungen*). On registration (*Immatrikulation*) each student receives an *Ausweiskarte*, which is his official identification (*Erkennungszeichen*) as a University student. The faculty consists of *ordentliche Professoren, Honorar-Professoren, außerordentliche Professoren, Dozenten* and *Lektoren*. Professors have *Lehrfreiheit*, that is, they have the privilege of lecturing (*lesen*) on any subject they consider appropriate; the students have *Lernfreiheit*, that is, they may attend any lectures they please or may cut class (*schwänzen*). There is no compulsory attendance (*Kollegzwang*), but in the final State examinations (*Staatsprüfungen*) the students are

89

required to show adequate knowledge of the subject matter of the required courses. A student who has not paid his fees (*Honorar*) is not permitted to attend lectures. Should he nevertheless come to the lecture hall (*Hörsaal*), he does so surreptitiously (*das betreffende Kolleg schinden*).

The oldest type of *Hochschule* is the *Universität*, which has a theological, law, medical, philosophical and science faculties. The chief universities are at Berlin, Bonn, Erlangen, Frankfurt-am-Main (a.M.), Freiburg im Breisgau (i.Br.), Greifswald, Halle, Hamburg, Heidelberg, Jena, Kiel, Köln, Leipzig, Mainz, Marburg, Münster in Westfalen (i.W.), Rostock, Tübingen and Würzburg. The head of the University is the *Rektor*, who bears the title of *Magnifizenz*. The heads of the faculties are the *Dekane*. The *Senat* (which decides questions dealing with University affairs) consists of the *Dekane* and several professors chosen for that purpose. The academic school year is divided into two semesters, the *Sommersemester*, from May to the end of July, and the *Wintersemester*, from November to the end of February. The summer vacation falls between the two semesters, i.e., from July to October (*die großen Ferien*), Easter vacation comes in March or April (*Osterferien*), and Christmas vacation (*Weihnachtsferien*) lasts two weeks.

At the end of eight semesters the student may register for the final examination (*Staatsprüfung*). Candidates in theology are examined by Church authorities; law students take two examinations (*Referendar* and *Assessor*) before a state board (*juristische Staatsbehörde*); philosophy students are examined by a special committee of professors (*wissen-*

schaftliche Prüfungskommission); and medical students take a preliminary examination called *Physicum* before being permitted to sit for the final *Staatsexamen.* A doctoral candidate is accepted only if he has at least six semesters at a German university. If the dissertation of a student of philosophy is accepted and he passes an oral examination, he receives the doctor's degree, *Dr.phil.* In some faculties the student can take a *Diplomprüfung,* which makes him a *Diplom-Chemiker, Diplom-Kaufmann,* etc.

Besides the University, there are other State *Hochschulen,* e.g., *Technische Hochschulen* (at Aachen, Berlin-Charlottenburg, Braunschweig, Darmstadt, Hannover, Karlsruhe, München, and Stuttgart) which give the degree of *Dr.Ing.* There are also *Hochschulen* for teacher training (*Lehrerbildung*), mining (*Bergakademien*), forestry (*Forstakademien*), art (*Kunstakademien*), music (*Musikhochschulen*), business (*Handelshochschulen*), and veterinarians (*tierärztliche Hochschulen*). There are also *Volkshochschulen* for adults, which require no prerequisites (*Vorkenntnisse*) and give no examinations.

B. In Austria

In general, the Austrian educational system is similar to the German. Among the *Mittelschulen* (secondary schools) comprising eight years of learning, with classes numbered from the first to the eighth (*erste, zweite, usw. bis achte Klasse*), the most important are the *Gymnasium* (classical school), *Realschule* (with stress on science, mathematics, and modern languages), and *Realgymnasium* (an intermediate form).

A special form of the latter is the *Arbeitermittelschule* (secondary school for workers) enabling gifted persons, at least seventeen years of age, who had to leave school after the eighth grade and have either completed their vocational training or already entered upon a vocational career, to resume their studies in order to attain the educational goal of a *Realgymnasium*. Classes are held, as a rule, in the evening hours.

While regular studies at a *Mittelschule* begin after the fifth grade of the *Volksschule* (public school), the *Aufbaumittelschulen* (reconstruction schools) make it possible for students who want to continue from the eighth grade to attain the same goal.

The *Bundeserziehungsanstalten* (Federal Education Institutions) have a similar aim, with the character of boarding schools. They are designed primarily for gifted children of underprivileged families.

There are two types of schools for commercial education: a two-year *Handelsschule* (School of Commerce) and a four-year *Handelsakademie* (College of Commerce). Graduates of the latter are admitted to the *Hochschule für Welthandel* (College of World Trade).

Apprentices in handicraft are obliged to attend a *Berufsschule* (Vocational School) during their three-year apprenticeship.

Persons who were prevented from engaging in the normal training for a college career but who, on the basis of their achievements in their later occupations, wish to round out their knowledge, are given a chance for adequate preparation for studies on the college level in their particular fields after passing a *Berufsreifeprüfung* (vocational maturity examination).

Austria has universities in Vienna, Graz and Innsbruck, and a Catholic Theological Seminary in Salzburg. The University of Vienna, founded in 1365, is the oldest University of the whole German-speaking area still in existence, and is divided into five *Fakultäten* (graduate schools): a *philosophische Fakultät* (roughly corresponding to a College of Liberal Arts in the American sense and covering a broad variety of sciences and humanities, with philosophy at the head of them all, required as one of the two major subjects at every *Rigorosum* or final examination of this school), a *medizinische* (School of Medicine), a *rechts- und staatswissenschaftliche* (School of Law and Political Sciences), a *katholisch-theologische* and an *evangelisch-theologische Fakultät* (Catholic Theological and Protestant Theological Seminaries). The average duration of the studies is five years. Then, after successfully passing his final rigorous examinations, the student is granted a doctor's diploma.

There are two *Technische Hochschulen* (Polytechnical Schools), in Vienna and in Graz, training the students in chemistry, applied mathematics, physics, and related sciences. They confer on the graduate student, after his passing two *Staatsprüfungen* (state examinations) the title of *Diplom-Ingenieur* (Diploma Engineer), and after some additional studies the title of *Doktor der technischen Wissenschaften* (Doctor of Engineering).

Besides these, there are a number of other graduate

schools: the *Hochschule für Bodenkultur* (College of Agriculture), the *Tierärztliche Hochschule* (Veterinary College) and the *Hochschule für Welthandel* (College for World Trade) in Vienna, and the *Montanistische Hochschule* (College of Mining) in Leoben.

C. Student Life

There are some characteristic differences of a general nature between life at German and American schools of higher education. In Germany and Austria school life on the high-school level is more restricted to the subjects of study in the narrower sense, less dedicated to sports and other extracurricular activities. University life, on the other hand, tends to be less rigid as to compulsory attendance of lectures and adherence to a systematic plan of studies. The final examinations and, in the case of the *philosophische Fakultät*, the dissertation, are what counts in the end. The closer concentration on school subjects (the important role football teams play at American colleges would be unthinkable in Germany) means that most students attain their doctor's degree at a somewhat earlier age than their American counterparts. This is also due to the fact that there are no such intermediate degrees as the bachelor's and the master's degrees to put a brake on the uninterrupted race for the coveted prize of the doctor's diploma.

The German student knows no hazing, proms or frats. The German *Studentenverbindungen* (Students' Associations), with their stress on rigid club rules, the *Kommers* (drinking bouts) and, in the case of *schlagende Verbindungen*, on fencing and dueling, bear only a faint resemblance to American fraternities. Since there is no campus and no dormitory, the German student has a private room in the city (*Bude*) where he is supposed to spend his evenings cramming for exams (*ochsen, büffeln*). After graduation and formal leaving (*Extramatrikulation*) when he goes forth into the cruel world (*Philisterium*) to practise his profession, he looks back with longing on the carefree days he spent at the University—and this is one thing he may have in common with all students the world over.

IX. TRAVEL HINTS

To go from one part of the city to another one may take a streetcar (*Straßenbahn*), a bus (*Autobus*) or a taxi (*Taxe* or *Mietwagen*). Besides these modes of transportation there is in Berlin an elevated train (*Hochbahn*) and a subway (*Untergrundbahn* or *U-Bahn*).

For longer trips into the country inquiries (*Erkundigungen*) should be made at a travel bureau (*Reisebüro*), which is generally situated near the railroad station (*Bahnhof*). Tickets (*Fahrkarten*) are bought inside the station from a ticket agent (*Schalterbeamter*), who must be told the destination, the class (there are three classes: *erste, zweite, dritte Klasse*), and one way or round trip—for example, *Hamburg, dritte, hin und zurück*. If one wishes to be insured for the trip, one asks for *Reiseunfallversicherung*.

The traveller then waits in the waiting room (*Wartesaal*) until the train arrives. When the train pulls in, he takes his baggage from the check room (*Gepäckabfertigung*) and following the sign *Zum Zuge* proceeds to the platform (*Bahnsteig* or *Perron*) and boards a *Personenzug*. A *Personenzug* may be a local (*Bummelzug*), or an express train which makes few stops or runs straight through without making any stops at all (*Eilzug, Schnellzug*). Such a *Schnellzug* may either be a train through which a passenger can walk freely from one coach to another (*Durchgangszug* or *D-Zug*), a train with a Diesel motor which makes a quick run between big cities (*Fliegender* or *F-Zug*), or a de luxe train (*Luxuszug* or *L-Zug*) with diner (*Speisewagen*) and sleeper (*Schlafwagen*).

After the signalman (*Signalwärter*) on the platform blows a whistle or waves a disk (*Scheibe*) and the conductor (*Schaffner* or *Kondukteur*) shouts *Alles einsteigen!* (All aboard!), the train pulls out. The passenger then takes a seat in a compartment (*Abteil* or *Coupé*) which may be reserved for smokers (*Raucher*) or for nonsmokers (*Nichtraucher*). After leaving the train the passenger must give up his ticket at the station exit (*Bahnsteigsperre*).

On entering or leaving the country the traveler is asked by the custom officials (*Zollbeamte*): *Haben Sie was Zollpflichtiges?* or *Haben Sie etwas zu verzollen?* (Have you anything to declare?); and if the traveler has only articles which are duty-free (*zollfrei*), a chalk mark (*Kreidezeichen*) is straightway put on his bags, and the custom procedure (*Zollabfertigung*) is over.

X. MONEY, WEIGHTS and MEASURES

1. Money (*Geld*)

   As a result of the currency reform (*Währungsreform*) after the war, the old money (*Reichsmark* RM) was exchanged at the rate of 10: 1 for the new (*Deutsche Mark* DM). 1 DM = 100 Pfennig.

2. The Metric System (*das metrische Maßsystem*). 1 *Meter* (written *m*) = 10 dm (*Dezimeter*) = 100 cm (*Zentimeter*) = 1000 mm (*Millimeter*). 1000 m = 1 km (*Kilometer*). 1 cm = approximately .4 inch. 1 m = $3\frac{1}{4}$ feet.

3. Weights (*Gewichte*)

   Das Gramm (written g). 1000 g is 1 *Kilogramm* (1 kg) or about 2.2 *Pfund* (2.2 pounds). 1 *Milligramm* (1 mg) = 1/1000 g). 50 kg = 1 *Zenter*. 100 kg = 1 *Doppelzentner*, *metrischer* or *Meterzentner*). 1000 kg = 1 *Tonne* (1 t).

4. Liquid Measures (*Hohlmaße*)

   Das Liter (written l). 100 l = 1 Hektoliter (hl). 1 l = approximately 1.1 quarts.

5. Time (*die Zeit*)

   The date (*das Datum*) is written as follows: 10. *Februar* 1954 or 10.2.1954.

   The hour is expressed as follows:

   It is 5: 15 (*es ist ein Viertel nach fünf; es ist ein Viertel sechs; es ist 5 Uhr* 15). The designation 17 *Uhr* 15 for 5: 15 p.m. is used by railroads, the post office, etc.

   It is 10: 30 (*es ist halb* 11; *es ist 10 Uhr* 30).

   It is 1: 45 (*es ist drei Viertel zwei: es ist Viertel vor zwei; es ist 1 Uhr* 45). *Es ist 13 Uhr* 45 means: it is 1: 45 p.m.

It is 7:20 (*es ist* 20 *Minuten nach sieben; es ist* 7 *Uhr* 20);
   es ist 19 *Uhr* 20 means: it is 7:20 p.m.
It is 11:40 (*es ist* 11 *Uhr* 40; *es ist* 20 *Minuten vor zwölf*);
   es ist 23 *Uhr* 40 means: it is 11:40 p.m.